Medieval Archaeology in the East Roman World

PAST IMPERFECT

See further
www.arc-humanities.org/our-series/pi

Medieval Archaeology in the East Roman World

Marica Cassis

British Library Cataloguing in Publication Data
A catalogue record for this book is available from the British Library

ISBN (PB): 9781641892193
e-ISBN (PDF): 9781802702026
e-ISBN (EPUB): 9781802702033

www.arc-humanities.org
Printed and bound in the UK (by CPI Group [UK] Ltd), USA (by Bookmasters), and elsewhere using print-on-demand technology.

Contents

List of Illustrations

Maps

In memory of my parents, Christos and Leslie Cassis, both of whom passed during the writing of this book.

Foreword

This book is the direct result of being asked repeatedly over the years where the church is at the site of Çadır Höyük. While I have worked there for twenty years now, we still have no evidence for the things we take for granted in East Roman archaeology: churches, elite housing, cemeteries. We have the messy remains of daily life, used and reused between the Late Roman and Seljuk periods. In my view, however, these are the remains that help us widen our scope from the more traditional, seemingly characteristic, elite and religious material culture of the period. It has taken me a long while to become comfortable with letting go of the traditional definitions of the period, but I hope here to illustrate just how important it is for us to do so if we are to fully come to grips with the Late Roman and medieval periods of the East Roman world.

In coming to these ideas, I have been supported by so many scholars, both in my field and in others. Sharon Steadman, Gregory McMahon, Jennifer Ross, and Burcu Yildirim have been my archaeological family for so long, and I continue to be grateful to them every single day. Endless important talks with Darlene Brooks Hedstrom, Fotini Kondyli, and Christian Raffensperger have helped me really come to terms with my own views of this material. John Haldon has been a friend and mentor. But I have also been helped by the approaches of others not in my field: I learned about modern historiography in the History Department at Memorial University of Newfoundland, where I first had to teach it, and I will be forever grateful to my colleagues there for introducing me to *The Midwife's Tale* by Laurel Thatcher Ulrich. At the University of Calgary, Lisa Hughes has helped me rethink space and Courtnay Konshuh has challenged me to think about wider medievalisms. Through his work in Indigenous worldviews, Craig Ginn has helped me understand how colonialism affects our research and our sense of privilege; he is also the kindest person I know. My students, graduate and undergraduate, challenge me every day not to accept old narratives, and everything I have learned from the people listed above—and many I have not—have helped me approach the East Roman world in new ways. And my family, Craig and Marsh, have kept me sane while I have done this work.

I'll write another book when we find the church.

Introduction

Eastern medieval archaeology is full of the impressive. From churches like the Hagia Sophia in Istanbul to museums full of glittering jewellery and golden icons, "Byzantium" in the popular imagination has taken on the trappings of the elite and religious. This tradition is wrapped up in northern European perceptions of the Near East, ones that go back to the crusades, and which were carried through the accounts of travellers to places like Istanbul and Jerusalem in the eighteenth and nineteenth centuries. Early scholarship mirrored this tendency, and much early academic work was dedicated to cataloguing and explaining the magnificent structures and objects of the Christian East.[1] Over the course of the twentieth century, multiple textbooks and museum catalogues have been dedicated to the study of the material culture of the Byzantine past, but until recently have primarily amplified our knowledge of the elite and the religious.[2] This has meant that what O. M. Dalton termed archaeology in 1911—

1 O. M. Dalton, *Byzantine Art and Archaeology* (Oxford: Oxford University Press, 1911) is, for example, one of the first systemic collections on Byzantine art and archaeology.

2 For example, Helen C. Evans and William D. Wixom, *The Glory of Byzantium: Art and Culture of the Middle Byzantine Era, A.D. 843–1261* (New York: Metropolitan Museum of Art, 1997) and Helen C. Evans, *Byzantium: Faith and Power (1261–1557)* (New York: Metropolitan Museum of Art, 2004).

which was, in large part, art historical in nature—has dictated the narrative of the study of Byzantine material culture for a very long time.

The focus on the impressive is, at first glance, not an obvious problem. After all, it sells museum tickets and textbooks; it is the first part of the East Roman world that most people encounter. Images of the Hagia Sophia and the words of Procopius are what bring students to our classes. Yet, in our focus on the elite and the beautiful, we have abandoned the majority of the population of the East Roman world to obscurity, ignoring, except among specialists, data which provides an important window into their lives. This book aims to change that narrative by introducing students to the field of non-monumental East Roman archaeology. My thesis is simple: East Roman archaeology has traditionally been understudied because it is difficult and largely unglamorous, but it needs to be better integrated into the larger fields of both medieval archaeology and East Roman studies because it provides insight into the pivotal transitional period between the ancient and early modern worlds. Through this we can trace the use and reuse of landscapes through environmental and population changes, and witness the cultural connectivity between newly integrated religious and cultural groups. The geographical focus ranges from Greece, through the Balkans and Anatolia, to the borders of Iran and North Africa but the contacts range beyond that, to Sicily, to Northern Europe, to China, to Africa.

It is a rich discipline with much scope for exploration, but it needs to be more fully integrated into the study of the medieval world and this book will, I hope, illustrate why that matters.

In order to do this, I have made several practical and theoretical decisions, as it is simply not possible to cover everything in such a short introductory text, but I hope that this will serve as a place for students to begin their exploration of *this* past. First, I have consciously abandoned the term Byzantine. As early as Dalton, scholars have been arguing about the appropriateness of this word. The term Byzantine, which

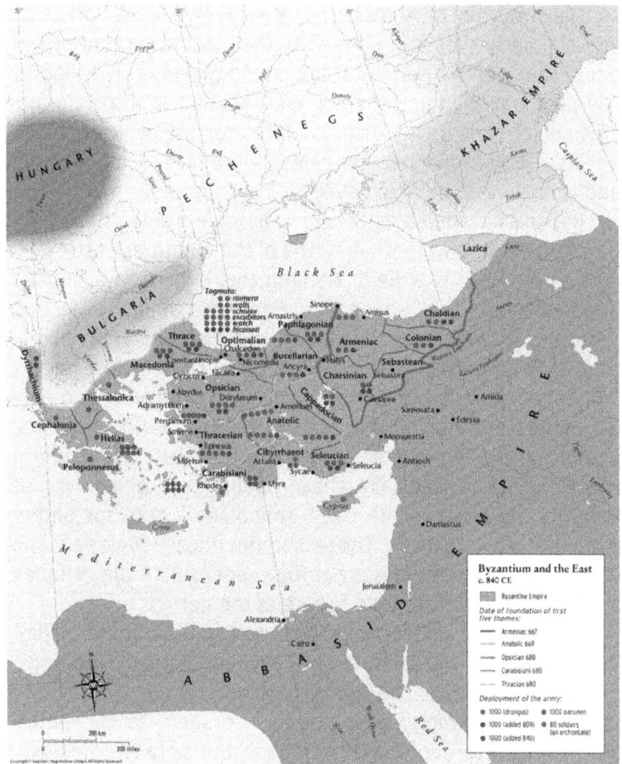

Map 1. Byzantium and the East. Created by Axiom Maps Ltd. Used with permission.

was a seventeenth-century invention of European scholars, assumes that a cultural and religious identity was shared over a vast chronological and geographical expanse. The term does not, and cannot, take into account variations in religious identity (such as the Syriac Christians of Eastern Anatolia); displaced and resettled populations (such as Bulgarians and Armenians); and Christian populations who lived alongside Muslim neighbours (as in Jerusalem or Syria, or along the southern border of Anatolia). The word Byzantine forces us into scholarly silos and undercuts the main argument of this book: that non-monumental archaeology shows us a deeply complex and changing society over the course of this period. This choice reflects my own scholarly training, which focused on Eastern Anatolia, northern Mesopotamia, and inland Syria, and is not one with which everyone will agree.

Byzantine studies as a field is grappling with these very problems right now, both in terms of the identities of the past and its identity as a field. Naming this book was a difficult undertaking for this reason. In the end, two things helped me decide how I wanted to approach the material. First, at the time of writing, many scholars (including myself!) are deeply influenced by the work of Anthony Kaldellis and his arguments for understanding the so-called Byzantine world under the name that these populations gave to their own world, which was *Romanía*.[3] Essentially, these people saw themselves as Romans. However, while the terminology works for understanding how many of these communities developed and viewed themselves, it does not fully encapsulate the complex interactions and formative nature of the period.

For me, the interactions *between* communities, including those who were influenced by East Roman traditions, but perhaps identified themselves differently, whether by language or theology, also need to be seen. To this end, I have chosen to capture this through the phrase "medieval archaeology" which has appeared increasingly over the past decade in relation to "Byzantine" archaeology. Medieval is a term that is very fluid, and can encapsulate both the Late

---

3 Anthony Kaldellis, *Romanland: Ethnicity and Empire in Byzantium* (Cambridge: Harvard University Press, 2019) for an important discussion of this issue. More recently, Anthony Kaldellis, *The Case for East Roman Studies* (Leeds: Arc Humanities Press, 2024). In some ways, East Roman can also be a problematic term, since material included in this book touches on places like Sicily and on populations that were distinctively not East Roman (like the Syriac Christians).

Roman period (primarily fifth and sixth centuries CE in the context of this book) and the subsequent period (up to about 1500). It has certainly been applied that broadly in European contexts. More importantly, however, the term allows for the inclusion of all of the communities—Christian, Muslim, Jewish, Persian—into the narrative without siloing them into artificial categories. Of course we must be clear about which community we mean at any given time, as well as the dates we are using, but it is my contention that the archaeology of the East Roman world and its surroundings needs better inclusion into the wider world of medieval archaeology. To that end, I will use both terms, East Roman and medieval, with explicit reference to geographical location and community identity.

Secondly, my approach in this book is explicitly theoretical in nature. The field of East Roman archaeology is relatively young, a discipline that sits at the crossroads of Late Roman, medieval, and Islamic archaeology, all of which initially grew out of Classical archaeology. Most medieval archaeology is a relatively recent invention, since prior to about the middle of the twentieth century, only cursory attention was given to the stratigraphical material that overlaid the Classical past.[4] There are a variety of reasons for this, most of which were connected to the interests and biases of Western scholars, something which will be further addressed in the first chapter. In short, this later material was often seen as representing a general decline in culture, and thus not particularly important. More theoretical models allow for more nuanced approaches to what remains.

The first theoretical movement reflected in this book is a focus on the spatial turn in archaeology.[5] This can be defined

---

4 Crow, "Archaeology," 47–58. Where a short-form citation is provided as the first reference to a work, please consult the Further Reading at the end for full details.

5 This is a notable addition in the medieval archaeology of both Europe and the East Roman world: Veikou and Nilsson, *Spatialities of Byzantine Culture from the Human Body to the Universe*. Veikou, Nilsson, and James, "(Byzantine) Space Matters! An Introduction," in

as the recognition that *all* space, from a built or rebuilt house to the landscape, is used and reused and can be interpreted to reflect an understanding of the social organization of a society (from politics to gender). This starting point widens our focus from *only* monumental architecture to any landscape that can be visibly identified with the medieval world, and has been a theoretical model in use in Western medieval archaeology since at least the 1980s. This theoretical shift is now appearing much more in East Roman archaeology, and is making an enormous impact on how we interpret space. In some cases, the focus has been on the medieval reuse of earlier, more impressive structures, and in others, it has been on more small-scale rural sites that have largely been underrepresented in the scholarship.

This is a significant shift because it brings to light new data as well as the complexities of different types of archaeology. For example, outside of monumental structures, both urban and rural archaeology are characterized by medieval reuse, which has complex stratigraphy that mirrors the intricacies of prehistoric archaeology. There are often no texts or sources to help clarify the material culture. Thus, this is the archaeology of small-scale changes and rebuilding—even within structures like churches and fortresses that started as major constructions. By recognizing the significance of this as lived space over long periods of time, we are able to reconceptualize what we know about the populations of the East Roman past who used and reused these structures.

In order to do this effectively, I turn explicitly to the field of microhistory and its archaeological outgrowth, singularity, as defined by the Icelandic school of microhistory.[6] This is an

Spatialities of Byzantine Culture, 8: "Because of the integral spatiality of social life (it all happens somewhere), all archaeologists—whether specializing with landscape and architecture or with material culture—deal with space even when they do not openly acknowledge it."

6 Magnússon, "Views into Fragments," and Mímisson and Magnússon, "Singularizing the Past." Peregrine Horden and Nicholas

approach to archaeology that has had considerable influence on my thinking. The core idea presented by Kristján Mímisson and Sigurður Gylfi Magnússon is that each archaeological site needs to be understood as an independent unit in order to stop archaeologists and historians from overgeneralizing our results to apply to an entire society. This does not mean that ultimately we cannot find trends but that the variation that exists in archaeological sites across geographical areas is reflective of different populations and/or different choices, and results in varying responses to their own space. Just as no two modern houses look the same, nor mean the same thing to their inhabitants, the same was true in the East Roman world. Thus, rather than starting with the historical narrative, as has been the tradition in East Roman archaeology, we start with the archaeological evidence, understanding the communities independently before we extrapolate to a wider picture or attempt to connect it to the written word.

A third theoretical movement which highly influences my approach to this material is that of environmental archaeology, some of which is hinged on landscape archaeology. Medieval archaeology in Europe was a forerunner in these discussions. The importance of landscape has been particularly key in the development of large survey projects which provide a more holistic view of land use over the *longue durée* and which have been used incredibly successfully in Greece and Türkiye particularly. Connected to this is the understanding that the landscape is a marker of environmental and climate change, and that rural sites provide us with a model for understanding how societies adapted and changed in the face of fluctuations in their environment.[7]

Purcell, *The Corrupting Sea: A Study of Mediterranean History* (Oxford: Blackwell, 2000) is also a pivotal text in understanding microregions.

7 Haldon et al., "The Climate and Environment of Byzantine Anatolia," 113–61, and McCormick et al., "Climate Change during and after the Roman Empire," 169–220.

All of these theoretical perspectives ultimately lead to the question of identities. As we reconsider space, site formation, and landscape, East Roman archaeology enters a discussion that is currently being undertaken in the larger field of Byzantine studies, as noted above.[8] East Roman archaeology is well poised to add to the discussion by illustrating the multiple identities which make up this world. These identities are tied to geographical locations; the urban/rural divide; expressions of Christianity; languages; and cultural expressions of self-identity. All of these play out in the choices people made in the past, which are then visible to us in the archaeological record but which need to be interpreted outside of only the narratives written by the elite and the religious. This is not to say that sources should be ignored, but it is important to recognize that the sources are non-existent or biased for the majority of the East Roman populations.

In order to illustrate the importance of thinking about location and population in determining identity, I have organized this book primarily around geographical categories, identifying problems and examples internal to each geographical area. In this way, I have tried to provide a coherent cross section of work and approaches. Chapter one deals with the problems that face the field as a whole, particularly around terminology, chronology, and categorization; it gets to the heart of the issues that we need to address by thinking about regionality. Chapter two focuses on Türkiye, because, as the home of Constantinople, it was the epicentre of the East Roman universe. However, rather than dealing with the more well-known sites of Asia Minor, I will focus on the importance of Anatolia in East Roman archaeology. Here we will deal with questions of multiple populations and the effects of colonialism on perceptions of the Eastern medieval world; we will also grapple with the question of how to identify resilience throughout the long medieval period, primarily through environmental evidence and rural communities. In chapter

8 Stewart, Parnell, and Whately, eds., *The Routledge Handbook on Identity in Byzantium.*

three, I move to Greece, where we consider the medieval as a locus of continuous landscape use, and pay particular attention to the importance of survey and the urban/rural divide. Greece provides a fascinating case study in continuity for East Roman archaeology. In chapter four, I question the separate identities of "Byzantine" and Islamic archaeology in the Levant, and consider the problems of categorization and borders in creating a holistic view of the East Roman and wider medieval world. Finally, in chapter five, we will look at medieval identities in the so-called liminal zones, including Mesopotamia, Cyprus, Sicily, Armenia, Central Europe, and Egypt, and question their isolation from the larger discussion of East Roman archaeology and their place in understanding regional identities. In each area I draw attention to archaeological work which exemplifies growth or stagnation in the field.

I will present controversies and problems, often with no solution, in order to illustrate the complexity of the field. Each geographical area discussed was influenced by the Roman past, the Christian present, and by their Muslim neighbours, but also by language, culture, and regionality. And each modern country grapples with how to integrate this history into their understanding of the past. In the end, this book cannot cover everything, but should serve as an introduction to both how we have traditionally thought about this archaeology, and new ways of moving forward in understanding the East Roman world. In providing an introduction to the kinds of questions that we should be asking of medieval archaeology, I am entering my plea that we begin to consider the significance of East Roman archaeology in the larger context of both medieval studies and world history. I am explicitly calling for us to be very careful about the kinds of terms and definitions we use, as these often limit our holistic understanding of the period and how it set the stage for the early modern world. The East Roman world provides a stunning entry into understanding the movements and coexistence of different peoples, religions, and cultures. The non-monumental archaeology has the potential to elucidate things like daily lives and rural populations that the written sources simply ignore.[9] The Hagia Sophia continues to be one of the most impressive structures in the history of this period but the farmhouses in rural Greece and Türkiye are perhaps just as important in telling us how everyone else lived.

---

9 Whittow, "Early Medieval Byzantium and the End of the Ancient World," 134–53.

Chapter 1

A Field with an Identity Problem

"Who in the world am I? Ah, that's the great puzzle!"
Alice in Wonderland, Lewis Carroll

It is almost impossible to provide a definition of East Roman archaeology with which everyone will agree. Regional differences affect our definitions of the period, as does the quantity, quality, and type of available evidence. All of this has its roots in the origins of the discipline, which had a serious impact on both accepted terminology for the field and on perceptions of the material culture of the East Roman world. This has made the field difficult to navigate. Unlike most archaeological disciplines, this particular branch of medieval archaeology did not begin from a clear foundational starting point. Rather, it developed out of the practical need of archaeologists to deal with post-Roman materials in Greece and the Near East. Overlaying this were the politics of, particularly, the late 1800s and early 1900s, which were rife with colonialism and Orientalism.[1] Non-monumental East Roman material is not glamorous, and was often characterized *only* in relation to the earlier Classical material, suggesting poorer, less advanced societies in the medieval period; this was combined with scholars explicitly only looking for the great cul-

1 Averil Cameron, "Byzantium's Place in the Debate over Orientalism," in *Languages and Cultures of Eastern Christianity: Greek*, ed. Scott Fitzgerald Johnson (London: Routledge, 2017), 533–45.

tures of the ancient world. The combination of these ideas was disastrous for the earlier years of this field, and thus in order to understand East Roman archaeology, we need to start by excavating the history of the discipline.

Origins

As noted, East Roman archaeology had its roots in, primarily, Classical art and archaeology, since the excavations of the great Greek and Roman cities uncovered sites that were overlaid with medieval material. However, the earliest manifestations of the field were through the study of the artistic traditions of the early Christian period, which was generally accepted to have begun with Constantine in the fourth century. The official acceptance of Christianity by Constantine was (and sometimes still is) seen by scholars as a watershed moment, when the pagan past gave way to Christianity. The period from the third to the sixth century was characterized by a distinctive art historical tradition of monumental churches, mosaics, paintings, and other decorative arts. While some of this artistic tradition was clearly a continuation of Roman norms (such as mosaics), already there was a sense among scholars that figural representations represented a decline in artistic tradition brought on by contact with the east.[2] Most archaeology was termed early Christian archaeology, primarily because of the concentration on churches and monasteries in these regions.[3]

Increased fieldwork in Greece and the Near East (primarily in Türkiye, the Levant, and Syria) in the early part of the

2 There were Orientalist debates about the quality of "Eastern" art, and the relationship to Christianity throughout the early part of the twentieth century. For example, see Josef Strzygowski, "The Origin of Christian Art," *The Burlington Magazine for Connoisseurs* 20, no. 105 (1911): 146–53.

3 For an excellent introduction to the history of the discipline, and its evolution to modern archaeology, see Caraher, Pettegrew, and Davis, eds. *The Oxford Handbook of Early Christian Archaeology*.

twentieth century helped expand the chronological scope of the material considered Early Christian, and this came to be defined by the term Byzantine, which was applied to material from the fourth century through to the fifteenth century, depending on location. The early approaches remained largely art historical, such as Dalton's *Byzantine Art and Archaeology*. While Dalton's text is an early summary, subsequent works continued to focus on large scale architectural remains, primarily Late Roman churches, and the beautiful religious art which characterized the elite in the Middle and Late Byzantine Empires. Surveys of the material culture were explicitly focused on art and monumental architecture,[4] and, while there was increasing interest in archaeology, it was still largely Late Roman and/or urban in focus. A notable example is the excavation of the Saraçhane in Istanbul, which uncovered the mosaics of the Great Palace. On the other hand, non-specialists who excavated earlier periods in (often) rural environments, quickly removed post-Classical finds and structures in order to get to the material below. It was often published sporadically (if at all), and very little analysis was done with most of it in these early years.

Many of the archaeologists digging these sites, particularly in the late nineteenth and very early twentieth century, were specialists in much earlier civilizations, and thus the medieval materials sometimes spanning the entirety of the Late Roman through to the Ottoman periods were not given full analysis. Moreover, much of this material was deemed unimportant because it was representative of populations (Late Roman, medieval, and early modern) that had lost the Classical or ancient past and were seen as degraded as a result. This was in large part an overt type of Orientalism that mirrored the concurrent colonial endeavours in the Near East. It became part of the narrative of the colonial powers that "the East" was degraded and that the colonizers had

4 David Talbot Rice, *Byzantine Art*, rev. ed. (London: Penguin, 1954); Richard Krautheimer, *Early Christian and Byzantine Architecture*, 3rd ed. (London: Penguin, 1979).

to save the great pre-medieval heritage for these communities.[5] Thus, in searching for the large and beautiful objects and cities in places like Ephesus, a great deal of overburden was simply removed. Indeed, "Byzantine" archaeology was born out of the material that needed to be removed to find the temples and the palaces of earlier centuries. As the defining characteristics of most of this archaeology were coarse wares and refurbished structures, a great deal of it was excavated poorly and with little real consideration for stratigraphy or publication.

The situation was exacerbated because many early Byzantine scholars then only used archaeology as a way to illustrate historical texts (a problem that was endemic to Classical archaeology of the period too). The written sources for the medieval world (particularly for the seventh to ninth century) are sparse, and Middle Byzantine period sources are largely concentrated on the elites of Constantinople or on religious accounts of saints. Further, linguistic differences separated Byzantine scholars from, for example, Syriac, Coptic, or Islamic scholars, creating divisions in our perception of the medieval world. It thus became easy to believe that the populations of the East Roman world outside of Constantinople had declined into invisibility and unknowability. This seemed to be confirmed by the nature of the finds that did come from the few sites that were explored. Gone were the caches of coins, except in rare circumstances, and the beautiful, imported wares. The stratigraphy instead presented locally made coarse wares and the ubiquitous bones of animals. Buildings were no longer of fine concrete or worked

---

5 See Lynn Meskell, "Imperialism, Internationalism, and Archaeology in the Un/Making of the Middle East," *American Anthropologist* 122, no. 3 (2020): 554–67 and the collection of articles in Lynn Meskell, ed., *Archaeology under Fire: Nationalism, Politics and Heritage in the Eastern Mediterranean and Middle East* (London: Routledge, 1998). The concept of Orientalism comes from Edward Said, *Orientalism*, who broadly argued that perceptions of the Middle East were largely constructs in biased Western approaches to the region.

stone, but, particularly in places like Türkiye and Greece, rough stones held together with packed mud. It is not difficult to see how the perception arose that this was a land time had forgotten.

Nevertheless, with time Classical archaeologists at sites like Athens and Ephesus became more interested in the Late Roman and medieval material that overlay these big Classical cities, and by the middle of the twentieth century, increasing attention was being paid to this data. The Late Roman material was still clearly identifiable as such, largely due to the prevalence of coins and the ubiquitous Late Roman red wares that are found all over the Late Roman world and which can be dated between the fourth and seventh centuries.

The subsequent centuries (seventh to ninth), however, were largely represented in archaeological contexts by less dateable remains: non-elite material culture such as coarseware ceramics and the loss of monumental urbanization as populations transitioned to a more rural post-Roman world.[6] What archaeologists found in the period after approximately the mid-seventh century was a changed environment, one where Classical materials were reused and repurposed for smaller, less elite populations.

Although the perceived decline of the cities began to appear earlier than the seventh century, it was the almost complete disappearance of *both* coins and red slip wares from many places in the seventh and eighth centuries which seemed to confirm it. The ubiquity of the material culture made it difficult to precisely date these stratigraphic levels. It also contributed to the sense of abandonment that came

---

6 Foss was one of the first archaeologists to recognize the significance of the decline of cities for our understanding of the urban transition between the Late Roman and medieval worlds. His early articles, including "The Persians in Asia Minor and the End of Antiquity," *The English Historical Review* 90 (1975): 721–47 and "Archaeology and the 'Twenty Cities' of Byzantine Asia," *American Journal of Archaeology* 81 (1977): 469–86 are compiled in Foss, *History and Archaeology of Byzantine Asia Minor.*

Figure 1. Red slip ware from Çadır Höyük. Courtesy of Çadır Höyük Excavations.

to characterize scholarly perceptions of these cities. In major urban centres like Athens and Constantinople, dedicated ceramicists and Byzantine experts were able to isolate and date some exceptions, like seventh century Constantinopolitan white wares, but in many East Roman sites, dateable fine wares disappeared almost completely. Since almost all of the archaeology took place in urban contexts until the latter part of the twentieth century, the idea of general societal decline was accepted for most contexts in the East Roman world.

These approaches then contributed to further problematic theories about the post-Roman world as a whole. In Türkiye and Greece, for example, archaeologists surveying older periods identified series of small hills which had medieval pottery (usually coarse wares) and small fortifications. These dated from this post-Roman period, and consequently were identified as small-scale fortifications for local peasants. They became, in the collective imagination, the hiding places of suffering peasants, locations where they gathered while, particularly, the Arab invaders passed in the late seventh and early eighth centuries. As Anderson has shown, though, this hardly does justice to the complicated stories of occupation in different parts of the Byzantine world.[7] Some of these sites, for example, were nowhere near the routes of the raiding parties sent over from the Islamic caliphates, and others, once excavated, proved to have been constructed as late as the twelfth and thirteenth centuries.

As I will show in the next chapters, these narratives are currently being rethought. The colonial origins of East Roman archaeology meant that, until recently, it has suffered from time-space compression, which has reduced a thousand years of history to a series of generalizations.[8] This term, which comes out of the work of historical geographers, means that in periods where little is known, we accept a certain amount of flattening of the history, both in terms of geography and chronology, in order to understand or explain them. For colonial archaeologists, medieval archaeological material (including East Roman and Islamic) was reduced to limited facts because they were deemed unimportant, degraded, and orientalized cultures. Limited archaeological exploration coupled with a lack of dateable ceramics and large architecture continued to obfuscate East Roman medieval archaeology, painting it all with the idea of decline. This is changing, but only with increased excavation and more theoretical understanding will we move away from these old narratives.

---

7 For an excellent discussion of the dating of these mounds, see Anderson, "The Medieval Afterlife of Ancient Mounds," in *Context and Connection: Studies on the Archaeology of the Ancient Near East in Honour of Antonio Sagona*, 359–79.

8 Barney Warf, *Time-Space Compression: Historical Geographies* (London: Routledge, 2008) posits that colonialism reduces our understanding of certain ancient cultures deemed less important by obfuscating cultural and temporal changes.

Whose Dates?

Compounding the problems identified above is the question of the dates we associate with the East Roman world throughout the medieval period. There is simply no consistency across the discipline. For many scholars, particularly those working in the Levant and Egypt, "Byzantine" begins with Constantine in the fourth century, with the shift of the empire to the east, and lasts until the mid-seventh century. In fact, it was Diocletian who moved the Roman capital east (and there were connections to Asia Minor even earlier than that), and many of the changes which would come to fruition in the Late Roman period had their origins in the late third century. As well, until at least the mid-seventh century, the traditions of the earlier Roman world remained firmly rooted in societies ranging from Spain to the borders of Iran. Although the term Late Antique was coined by Peter Brown to capture the unique nature of this period, particularly in the West, it remained very much the Roman world, as Anthony Kaldellis has shown.[9] So, rather problematically, different scholars refer to the earliest period by all three terms: Early Byzantine, Late Roman, and Late Antique, and there is simply no consistent definition for what we mean when we use these terms, and what dates we can all agree on.

Determining when to end the period is also controversial. For some scholars, it was the arrival of Islam which pushed the Arabs into the Levant, Egypt, and to the borders of Anatolia. For others, the end of what is known as the Roman Warm Period between 400 and 500 CE led into a cold period that was roughly linked to the post-650 period. Archaeologists working in different areas cope with this terminology in varying ways. For scholars working in Roman or Byzantine archaeology in the Levant, the dates seem simple enough. The arrival of the Arabs is, for obvious reasons, accepted as a significant breaking point in this region particularly. Indeed, there is no purely

---

9 Peter Brown, *The Making of Late Antiquity* (Cambridge: Harvard University Press, 1978).

"Byzantine" archaeology after 650, and instead we see the term Islamic archaeology used. However, archaeology continues at Jewish and Christian sites like Madaba for this later period. The term Byzantine largely disappears from places like Israel, Jordan, and Egypt, unless in conjunction with Christian churches, and even then, these are often classified by specific Islamic caliphates, such as the Umayyad period. The archaeology, then, often runs along religious lines, and in many ways obfuscates the continuity and interaction between communities. It is my contention that medieval archaeology is a much more useful term for this archaeology, as it allows us to capture all of the populations that existed in the Levant without creating false dichotomies between religious groups *where they are not necessary.*[10]

For places like Greece and Türkiye, on the other hand, the use of the term "Byzantine" extends for a much longer time. Late Roman and Early Byzantine are used interchangeably by some scholars to refer to the period between the fourth and seventh centuries, while others reserve Early Byzantine for the period between the seventh and the ninth centuries (previously known as the Dark Ages). This later period is particularly difficult to define because of the lack of written sources and excavated sites. Nevertheless, for many of us, archaeologically speaking, the period between the seventh and the ninth century marks something remarkably different from what preceded it.[11] We now understand that this difference was caused by a number of factors, including the arrival of the Arabs *and* environmental changes. The period can be more properly defined as the response of communities to change, as opposed to passively encountering external events.[12] In fact, I would argue that this is precisely where

---

10 For further discussion of the multiplicity of communities, see Avni, *The Byzantine-Islamic Transition in Palestine*.

11 Bintliff, *The Complete Archaeology of Greece Century AD*, 382 for a similar discussion.

12 See for example John Haldon, "'Cappadocia Will Be given over to

we see the start of a true medieval archaeology of the East Roman world. While there are hints of it in the lead up to about 600 CE, it is this period at the end of the Late Roman era through to the mid-ninth century that creates a window for domestic change and intercultural and interreligious interaction that differentiates the period from what came before.

The overall trend in this period was a shift to smaller villages and a more rural environment, but it is too deterministic to attribute these changes to one event or another on a large scale. The determination of the so-called decline of the region, what led to the term "the Dark Ages," was largely a combination of the lack of archaeology with a plethora of contemporary religious primary sources that saw the arrival of Islam through an apocalyptic lens. Yet, increasingly, archaeological exploration now shows that the East Roman world was not abandoned, but rather changed to something more rural and local even within urban contexts.[13] This can be seen, by the way, in *some* of the written sources from the period, including several Syriac chronicles and hagiographies—sources that have not always been taken into account in this discussion due to the language barrier.

More is known about the medieval periods in Greece and Western Anatolia after the ninth century, largely because church building becomes more prominent again and, in much of Greece and the coastal areas of Asia Minor, imported ceramics again become visible. Urban centres reassume increased importance, although much less so than in the Late Roman period. Nevertheless, these urban areas allow for a better chronology for the mid-ninth through to the start of the thirteenth century. Additionally, much more is written about what is termed the Middle Byzantine period, which

Ruin and Become a Desert': Environmental Evidence for Historically-attested Events in the 7th–10th Centuries," in *Byzantina Mediterranea: Festschrift für Johannes Koder zum 65*, ed. Klaus Belke (Vienna: Böhlau, 2007), 215–30.

13 Roberts et al., "Not the End of the World? Post-Classical Decline and Recovery in Rural Anatolia," 305–22.

gives a perhaps false sense of security in understanding these societies. In fact, little is known about the rural medieval communities of Anatolia and Greece, precisely (again) because they are not in the written sources and because few have been excavated. So, while elite and religious society is clearer for this period, much remains to be said about the ordinary people and their lives.

This can also be said for the late medieval, or late Byzantine period, which lasts roughly from the early thirteenth century through to the fall of Constantinople in Anatolia, and which extends longer in Greece. This is a period of fragmentation as the world changed once again. What remains problematic about this is the terminology that restricts our understanding to only the Christian populations that identified with the Orthodox in Constantinople (more on this in chapter five); such terminology leaves out the cultural and religious interactions that occurred in both the Middle and Late Byzantine periods. The inhabitants of both urban and rural worlds, for example, interacted with different groups of Christians and Muslims, from as far away as Rus and Scandinavia to the north, and Mongolia to the east. Yet the term Byzantine centralizes, once again, Constantinople (and other urban centres), leaving other medieval areas in a liminal space. It also leaves out those who continued to identify as Roman living under, for example, Seljuk rule in Anatolia or Latin rule in Greece.[14] We need to start seeing these periods as not just representing one group of people but rather a people who were interacting in a global context with all manner of cultures and religions. To this end, we need to see this period more properly as medieval.

---

14 One notable exception to this is Speros Vryonis, *The Decline of Medieval Hellenism in Asia Minor and the Process of Islamization from the Eleventh through the Fifteenth Century* (Berkeley: University of California Press, 1971). While an important contribution that is one of the only works to consider this populations, this book must be used critically due to inherent biases about the arrival of the Turks.

Whose Culture?

Connected to the problem of dates is the problem of geography. Here too the boundaries get fuzzy, and this is another place where we need to consider shifting to the more inclusive concept of a medieval archaeology. As we have seen, the difficulties with terminology and dating means that there is no consistency between geographic regions, and that the terminology creates unnecessary boundaries in a world that was much more fluid in practice. Scholars have increasingly been showing the importance of groups that sit in what we would term the liminal zones of the medieval world, and our current definitions (Byzantine, Islamic) create barriers that make it difficult to situate these groups. As noted above, this is a particular issue in understanding how Islamic and Christian communities operated in conjunction with one another. In the Levant and Egypt, this involves Christians, Muslims, and Jews living beside one another, while for places like Anatolia, in also involves interactions over borders. But even before the arrival of the Muslims, we need to consider interactions between the East Roman world and the Sasanians in Persia. The lasting legacy of this interaction can be seen in monuments like the Great Palace mosaics and the Dome of the Rock, but also in the churches in Eastern Anatolia.

Less obvious, perhaps, are the communities which existed linguistically and theologically on the edges of empire. These people were often seen as separate groups, and thus not generally included in Byzantine history, yet were integral to the wider medieval period. This includes, for example, the Syriac Christians of Eastern Anatolia, northern Mesopotamia, Iraq, Iran and even as far as the Persian Gulf, all of whom had contact with or were part of the East Roman world. Egyptian Coptic Christians, as well, were in touch with both Orthodox and Syriac Christians (see chapter five), and Armenian Christianity was heavily influence by both types of Christianity. More recent work has been done on the Rus, the Balkans, and Byzantine Italy, but these groups *still* remain on the sidelines of the overall Eastern medieval narrative. While linguistic differences have made it difficult for historians to cross between the texts, particularly since so many works in Armenian and Syriac have not been translated into modern languages, this is not true for the archaeology and material culture, which can provide evidence for connections and commonalities between communities. Yet, we are bound by the old narratives of different theological and linguistic groupings. This limits our ability to understand the whole region, because it creates an artificial sense of segregation between these groups.

This, then, provides another reason for moving away from the categorizations that we have used for so long, as they keep us from seeing how and where interaction occurred between communities. It also allows us to believe in a monolithic Byzantine religious identity, which really never existed. A community in Eastern Anatolia, for example, had far more in common with a Syriac community in northern Mesopotamia, than either did with Constantinople; both are part of the East Roman milieu. The archaeology shows precisely the kinds of commonalities that existed through parallel ceramics and small finds, through regional artistic trends, and through the presence of different religious groups living within travelling distance of one another. Further, travel and contact is witnessed in the archaeological remains through the presence of things like pilgrim flasks and camel bones. Mostly this kind of interaction is witnessed if we move away from overdependence on elite and religious objects that reflect a particular type of identity, and consider a medieval East Roman archaeology that includes everyone. The medieval Eastern world was as complex and as global as our own, albeit on a different scale.

Where Do We Go from Here?

As I see it, the solution to such issues of identity is to embrace the complexity, rather than try to categorize it. East Roman archaeology is a field in flux as scholars grapple with the damage done by colonialist and Orientalist traditions in the wider field of archaeology, as well as the tendency of traditional scholars to privilege the art of the elite and the religious. Two approaches that will serve us well are an embrace of theoretical perspectives and the use of microhistories.

Theoretical approaches allow us to ask different questions of different populations. The spatial turn, as noted in the introduction, brings us into contact with how space was utilized over time. This allows us to think about how different people lived and interacted with space, both internal and external, both the built environment and the landscape. It also allows us to think about the interaction between climate and people, and how each affected the other. As the rest of the book will show, different theoretical models have been used in different geographical locations, and we can learn from each other about the kinds of questions we should be asking. For example, in many parts of the Near East, churches have been systematically catalogued several times (Cilicia and Isauria, the Tur Abdin, Syria), but little has been said about the villages that surround them. In Greece, however, much more work has been done on precisely that subject. In Anatolia, climate is a major consideration, largely because of the proxy environmental data available to medieval archaeologists. The questions we ask can be applied to places like Egypt or Armenia as well. In short, we need to be open to different questions, even of seemingly well-understood structures and places.

Microhistory offers a way forward with these questions. For a long time, Byzantine archaeology has been led by questions from the written sources. This has often meant that entire regions have remained silent. Taking each site and establishing its chronological stratigraphical history *before* turning to sources (if they exist), allows us to establish a baseline before we fall victim to the narratives about decline and abandonment. Each site has to be seen for its own evidence; this allows us to understand what its unique influencers and developments were, before being put into context with other sites. In short, it allows for an East Roman archaeology. The variations between two sites, even when they are within walking distance of one another, allows us to understand the variations in human existence in the medieval period, and from there extrapolate to the wider narrative of the period.

This is such a rich field. Contained within the fourth to fifteenth centuries are the evolution of the Roman Empire, the rise of the Islamic world, and the cultural and religious pluralism that characterizes the modern Middle East. While "Byzantine archaeology" has become weighed down by the labels of the past, rehabilitating it as medieval East Roman archaeology allows us to understand its role as a fundamental period of transition and interaction, and provides a stepping stone to understanding how the Middle East developed as it did.

Chapter 2

Anatolia: A Case Study in Resilience

The 2011 film *Once Upon a Time in Anatolia*, directed by Nuri Bilge Ceylan, follows a group of men looking for a body on the Anatolian Plateau. The film is haunting, and as the characters move from the fields to villages, it becomes clear that the landscape is as much a character in this film as any of the people. At first glance, the rolling hills and rocky outcrops seem barren and abandoned. Around each corner, however, is a story; at one point, an ancient carved face appears out of the rock on a windy night. What seems empty is peopled by the continuity between past and present lives, and this history resounds through these villages and fields in small ways. Indeed, it is precisely the smallness of the people and their actions in the vast timelessness of the landscape which makes this film so powerful.

Understanding the medieval world in Anatolia unfolds in many ways like this film. The stories are small and hidden, but when we as archaeologists deconstruct the finds and the sites, we can uncompress time and space, and the medieval period rolls out as one of varied and continuous habitation. This has to be done through a series of microhistories, as often excavated sites are separated by vast amounts of space. However, when we lay the stories of each site side by side, two common characteristics become evident. First, the use of each site is both unique and complex; second, each individual site shows how local populations adapted to shifting environments. Medieval archaeology in Anatolia unfolds, then, like a series of slow and complex stories that are ultimately all connected by the land.

I argue here that a microhistorical approach provides insight into the lived realities of ordinary communities, visible through their ceramics, their reuse of architecture, and their use of space to reflect localized needs. Perhaps most importantly, it also shows the response of such communities—successful or not—to changing climate. Medieval archaeologists working in Anatolia are at the forefront of this discussion of resilience, one that has pressing importance for our modern age.

History of the Field

The scholarly approach to East Roman archaeology in Türkiye has been varied since its origins as a field of study in the late 1800s, and this has affected the growth of the discipline. Roughly speaking, the data can be categorized in three ways. First, there are chronological surveys of art and architecture which present typologies of mostly churches, fortifications, and religious material culture. This type of work dates back to Dalton (1911), carried through to Richard Krautheimer (1979), and was most recently updated by Robert Ousterhout (2019). Ousterhout's work is particularly important in his recognition of the importance of geography in the regional development of East Roman architecture, as well as his preference for the term medieval. Nevertheless, secular and/or rural architecture as a whole remains poorly understood in the historical surveys of the architecture of the East Roman world.

Beginning around the turn of the twentieth century, a second category of material appeared. These were surveys of churches in various regions of Asia Minor and Anatolia; most prominent among these were those of Gertrude Bell and William Ramsay. These regional studies have continued, and provide insight into ecclesiastical architecture in particular regions such as Cilicia and Constantinople.[1] By the mid-twentieth century, similar surveys, this time focused on

1 For example, Stephen Hill, *The Early Byzantine Churches of Cilicia and Isauria* (Aldershot: Variorum, 1996).

fortifications began to appear.[2] Perhaps most importantly, the *Tabula Imperii Byzantini* series out of Vienna began in 1976 as a means of recording Byzantine sites through survey (often in conjunction with written sources) throughout the Byzantine themes.[3] In all cases, although archaeological analysis is employed, the focus remains on the standing (and thus primarily religious and elite) architecture and often privileges sites with corresponding textual references. The major limitation of these approaches, particularly in the early examples, has been that the wider context of the structures was often not taken into account, largely because no excavation was undertaken. So, even when structures stand within villages (as in the Tur Abdin in Eastern Anatolia), the focus was solely on the large structures.

The final category is, of course, excavation and survey. As early as the late nineteenth and early twentieth centuries, archaeologists began to record the finds from medieval stratigraphical levels (roughly 600 to 1500 CE). As noted earlier, however, most of the first scholars excavating major sites were interested in earlier material. Along the coast of Asia Minor, early excavations at places like Ephesus were focused on the Classical material, and so there was only sporadic recording of the Late Roman and medieval remains. In Anatolia, archaeological exploration was often focused on Hittite and Assyrian civilization, with the same result. In some cases data was recorded and kept and archaeologists are now recognizing that archives contain more data than made it into the final reports. To that end, there has been a successful

---

2 Clive Foss and David Winfield, *Byzantine Fortifications: An Introduction*, vol. 22 (Pretoria: University of South Africa, 1986). A more recent updating of this material: N. D. Kontogiannis, *Byzantine Fortifications: Protecting the Roman Empire in the East* (Havertown: Pen & Sword, 2022).

3 While physical books are still produced, they have now moved to a digital model: *Tabula Imperii Byzantini*, https://tib.oeaw.ac.at/, July 9, 2024.

turn towards archival archaeology to try to uncover more of this data from turn-of-the-century projects.

By the middle of the twentieth century, there was much more dedicated interest in, particularly, the Late Roman material in the urban centres on the coast of Asia Minor. This period saw important work done at major Classical cities like Ephesus, Assos, Pergamum, Miletus, among others, as well as concentrated work at sites like Anemurium, Alahan, and a number of other sites on the southern coast of Anatolia. Many of these excavations focused on tracing the evolution from the Roman through to the Late Roman period, and it is out of these excavations (particularly at Ephesus) that Clive Foss developed his theory of decline. As Late Roman cities lost the ability to fund their infrastructure, something that is well known from legal and economic history, a number of sites began to show stagnation, decline, reuse, and restructuring. What has become clear, however, is that the changes were not as quick or as stark as we have previously believed. There is a far more complex story of reuse and resilience which has become clearer in more recent excavations and survey (as I will discuss below).[4]

Anatolia remained largely unknown, however, until the last twenty years or so, when increasingly important work has focused on the Late Roman and medieval levels of sites that are known primarily as Bronze or Iron Age excavations. Thus, for example, medieval excavations have been carried out at places like Boğazköy (Hattusha), Sinope, and Kilise

---

4 This is in stark comparison to more recent work on the Late Roman and Byzantine remains at various sites. For example, Sabine Ladstätter, "Ephesus," in *The Archaeology of Byzantine Anatolia*, ed. Niewöhner, 238–48. Careful consideration of the Late Roman material has led to a redating of the so-called abandonment levels, pushing them further into the late seventh century through a consideration of the reuse of artifacts like coins. Similarly, work at Assos by Beate Böhlendorf-Arslan has shown a strong urban culture during the sixth century: "The Glorious Sixth Century in Assos," in *Asia Minor in the Long Sixth Century*, ed. Ine Jacobs and Hugh Elton (Philadelphia: Oxbow, 2019), 223–45.

Tepe. Revolutionary work on the early medieval period has been carried out at Amorium and Euchaïta (Avkat) in Anatolia, and Byzantine and Seljuk period excavations are the focus at Komana (near Tokat). There are a number of smaller salvage sites as well, particularly in the far east of Anatolia, that have had careful excavation of the medieval levels, which are less well-known but no less important. These include sites like Sos Höyük, Tille Höyük, and Gritille, which provide stratigraphic levels of medieval habitation which parallel others in Anatolia, such as Çadır Höyük.

It is worth noting that there is a parallel lacuna in the field of early Seljuk archaeology in Anatolia as well. Once again, while much is known about the elite schools, hospitals, and mosques in cities like Konya and Sivas, little is known about the role the Seljuks played in the rural environments they took over between the eleventh and thirteenth centuries. While Seljuk finds are invariably found at small sites like Çadır Höyük, the role of non-elite Turkic peoples is poorly understood in the overall narrative of the arrival of the Seljuks in Anatolia. While important work has been done recently on Seljuk art and archaeology with a view to reintegrating them into the history of the region, this period suffers from the same problems that have traditionally beset East Roman archaeology. The connection and transition between the Christian medieval and Islamic Seljuk periods—arguably the era that first helped to construct modern Türkiye—is still poorly understood and needs to be fleshed out more substantially through inclusion in the wider narrative of medieval excavation.

All three categories outlined above hold important status in our approach to East Roman medieval archaeology. What archaeologists are recognizing now is that it is imperative that we combine all of this data, as well as textual and inscriptional material, to create a holistic approach to the period and the region. Because of the disparate nature of the data, the most useful way to do this is to consider each area as a microhistorical case study. By tracing the population between the fifth and fifteenth centuries at each site (where feasible), we can see how these communities adapted and changed within local contexts without worrying about overriding imperial narratives.

Microhistories and Environment in Anatolia

Ideas of decline, abandonment, and collapse have all played a significant role in the narratives of, particularly, East Roman studies. Early responses to known environmental changes equated the so-called fall of Rome with the climate change that began at the end of the Roman warm period (ca. 400 CE), and the subsequent decline of the cities in the sixth century. The resurgence of the Middle Byzantine Empire, as seen through increased monumental architecture and literature, has been connected to the Medieval Warm Period (ca. 950–1250); this was in turn followed by severe droughts and famine when the climate failed after that date (the Little Ice Age). However, reality is always more complex than simple causation, and such broad frameworks need to be nuanced; societal changes are the result of interactions of environmental, social, and political changes. People adjust and adapt to changes in environment, and as John Haldon has said in a recent article deconstructing the notion of collapse, "Human actions need to be understood in terms of their "timescape," the ways in which social praxis and perceptions are embedded within a context of continuing social processes functioning at a variety of temporal and spatial scales."[5] In short, we need to understand that site formation was affected by both environmental and anthropogenic factors working in tandem with one another in order to understand the survival and resilience of communities in Anatolia.

One of the key movements in East Roman archaeology at the time of writing is in interdisciplinary work around envi-

---

5 John Haldon et al., "Demystifying Collapse: Climate, Environment, and Social Agency in Pre-Modern Societies," *Millennium* 17, no. 1 (November 9, 2020): 1–33 at 4. See also the Climate Change and History Research Initiative spearheaded by John Haldon at Princeton: https://climatechangeandhistory.princeton.edu/, July 9, 2024.

ronmental archaeology and the concepts of sustainability, adaptability, resilience, and collapse as they apply to medieval settlements. This work has been initiated by scholars who recognize the importance of using scientific environmental evidence such as climate modelling and pollen core samples to supplement the archaeological and historical material. What the environmental data shows is a far more complex story than simply decline; it shows massive variation in the resilience of communities in adapting to climate fluctuations. Publications by Michael McCormack, John Haldon, and Neil Roberts, among others, illustrate a complicated relationship between the environment and human agency during the Late Roman and medieval periods that reinforce the need for a microhistorical approach to archaeological sites.[6] While the environment had an effect on societies, it is, in reality, the reaction of societies to this environmental change—their resilience and adaptability—that allowed communities to change and evolve. This then connects to resilience theory, which comes out of the environmental sciences, and sees human societies as moving in a continuum of growth, conservation, release, and reorganization.[7]

However, this has to be nuanced in relation to the evidence from each site. For example, in Anatolia, the responses to environmental change at Çadır Höyük, which showed remarkable resilience, were substantially different from Euchaïta, which contracted substantially after the seventh century.

This understanding of the environmental responses has also allowed archaeologists to better understand the interactions between people and their local environments. To this end, East Roman archaeologists more routinely focus our analysis on three defining characteristics of East Roman

---

6 McCormick et al., "Climate Change during and after the Roman Empire," 169–220; Roberts et al., "Not the End of the World?"; Haldon et al., "The Climate and Environment of Byzantine Anatolia," 113–61.

7 Lance H. Gunderson and C. S. Holling, *Panarchy: Understanding Transformations in Human and Natural Systems* (Chicago: Island, 2012).

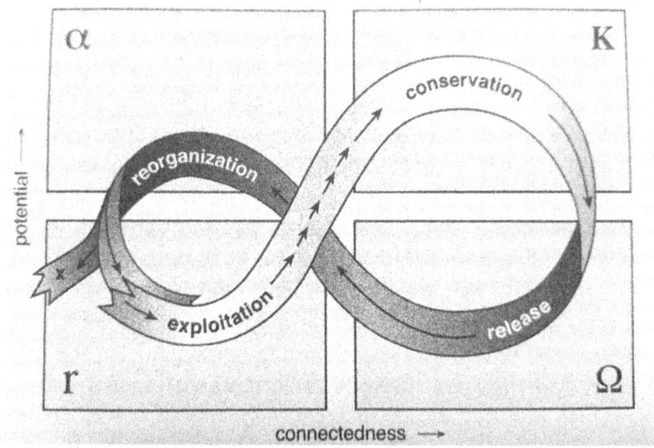

Figure 2. Stylistic view of ecosystems functions.
From Lance H. Gunderson and C. S. Holling, eds., *Panarchy: Understanding Transformations in Human and Natural Systems* (Washington: Island, 2002).
Reproduced by permission of Island Press.

archaeology: reuse and rebuilding; ceramics analysis; and the social dynamics of domestic architecture. First, older Roman and Late Roman structures were often reused and/or rebuilt in less ostentatious ways. Older structures that had fallen into disrepair (such as amphitheatres) were often taken apart for building materials, and large buildings were reused for housing, stables, and temporary shops, starting at the end of the Late Roman period. Houses were rebuilt several times, and sometimes subdivided to accommodate multiple families, or combined housing and commerce/industry. Such reuse is often difficult to define archaeologically without careful stratigraphic work, and in early excavations was often completely missed, or seen in a negative light as simply a sign of decline. However, as noted above, excavations at Assos and Ephesus have made it clear that this model is too simplistic.

A second focus of analysis involves better understanding of East Roman medieval ceramics. In some places, like Greece, more progress has been made in chronology and seriation, while in others, like Anatolia, much work is yet to be done. The ceramics assemblage for the Roman and Late Roman period (until the mid seventh century) is fairly well understood. These dates are largely based on the presence of red slip wares, both the original African Red Slip wares that originated in Tunisia, and imitation wares that were produced in different centres all over the Mediterranean. With the disruptions in trade networks during the seventh century, workshops for red slip wares died out in many places, and there was an increase in the production of locally made coarse wares throughout the medieval Mediterranean.[8] The disappearance of the ubiquitous red slip wares left a gap in the archaeological record, because in most places outside of major urban centres, it was not replaced by other clearly dateable glazed wares until the ninth and tenth centuries. Although there *are* plain glazed wares and glazed white wares after the seventh century, these do not appear in great quantities in most inland locations; rather, between particularly the seventh and ninth centuries, coarse wares are the constant. These ceramics are almost impossible to date with any precision outside of stratigraphic analysis because they are usually made from local clays and are common forms (like cooking pots). The interchangeability of these vessels contributed to the impression of decline and abandonment, as did the fact that their appearance was concurrent with the decline in coinage at many sites.

---

8 The standard texts on these wares are John W. Hayes, *Late Roman Pottery* (London: British School at Rome, 1972). See also Joanita Vroom, *Byzantine to Modern Pottery in the Aegean: 7th to 20th Century: An Introduction and Field Guide*, 2nd ed. (Turnhout: Brepols, 2014). Through various excavations it has become clear that, contrary to earlier beliefs, red slip wares lasted into the seventh century at many sites.

Finally, archaeologists are now increasingly turning to secular architecture such as domestic habitations in order to consider both the structures themselves, and to theorize about the social dynamics and life courses of the people who utilized them. This is relatively uncharted territory, but as increased work is done in Asia Minor and Anatolia more can be said about these structures. For Constantinople, much has been written on palaces and elite housing, and this has largely become the standard for the field.[9] However, increasingly we are focusing on rural and non-elite sites. Efforts have been made to classify and explain them in the works of, particularly Kim Bowes and Simon Ellis,[10] but more work needs to be done to understand vernacular housing in sites in rural Anatolia, particularly in the period after about 700 CE, where the remains of Roman-style villas disappear. Understanding these structures also allows us to use theoretical perspectives like gender theory to consider how such localized societies utilized space to enact social and domestic norms, and to consider the lives of the populations themselves.

As we move to two case studies from Sagalassos and Çadır Höyük, I will stress again the microhistorical approach. Both sites provide important evidence for the use of environmental, ceramic, and theoretical archaeology, but it is important to not overstate the parallels. That is, each one reflects a specific community. But what is constant is the human agency involved in keeping communities resilient. Not only does this approach provide a way of understanding the East Roman communities, but it can be further posited to include the arrival of the poorly documented Turkic groups on

---

9 Albrecht Berger and Philipp Niewöhner, "Residential Constantinople," in *The Cambridge Companion to Constantinople*, ed. Sarah Bassett (Cambridge: Cambridge University Press, 2022), 150–65.

10 Kimberly Diane Bowes, *Houses and Society in the Later Roman Empire*, Duckworth Debates in Archaeology (London: Duckworth, 2010); Simon Ellis, *Roman Housing* (London: Duckworth, 2000); Simon P. Ellis, "The End of the Roman House," *American Journal of Archaeology* 92, no. 4 (1988): 565–76.

Figure 3. View from Sagalassos. Photograph by author.

the Plateau, as many of those communities are visible within the medieval narrative as well.

Sagalassos[11]

Located in southwestern Anatolia in historical Pisidia, Sagalassos was a city with a history dating back to the Hellenistic period. While the majority of excavations at Sagalassos have focused on the extensive monumental Roman remains, more recent work has uncovered more of the Late Roman and medieval remains both at the site and in the surrounding area (primarily through survey). Sagalassos has increasingly become an important case study for understanding continuity of settlement in medieval Anatolia, and the excavators have been able to tackle all of the problems isolated above:

---

11 Marc Waelkens, "Romanization in the East: A Case Study: Sagalassos and Pisidia," *Istanbuler Mitteilungen* 52 (2002): 311–68 for a good introduction to this period; newly published is Jeroen Poblome, ed., *Documenting Ancient Sagalassos: A Guide to Archaeological Methods and Concepts* (Leuven: Leuven University Press, 2023).

reuse, ceramics, and continuity into the eleventh and twelfth centuries (and even later).

Early explorations of the site suggested that Sagalassos followed the pattern established by Foss (discussed above), and scholars initially posited that after two devastating earthquakes and successive rounds of plague, the city fell into disrepair and was largely abandoned. More recent work has nuanced this, showing that there is substantive evidence for rebuilding and reuse that reflected changing uses of space after the start of the sixth century.[12] Nevertheless, the initial narrative ran as follows. After the first earthquake at the start of the sixth century, effort was made to rebuild parts of the destroyed central parts of the city. Some of this work was never finished, a result of the plague which hit the city about forty years later. However, during the sixth century, various types of encroachment and subdivision resulted in the repurposing of parts of the Agora particularly, illustrating new types of commercial and domestic use in this space.

The excavators now indicate a more complex understanding of the changes. The Lower Agora was largely abandoned, while the central area showed a move to more commercial and workshop activity (which is often visible when buildings are subdivided). However, some rebuilding occurred in the Upper Agora, and, at the same time, other structures in the city—including a wealthy house—were rebuilt with expensive components. While it is clear that by the end of the sixth century, the use of some of the formerly imperial spaces was changing to reflect a more localized population with changing needs, neither all wealth nor populations disappeared from the city as evidence for elite structures continued past this period. These subsequent levels reflected more local organization and focus, which was paralleled by declining imported goods. A second earthquake, this time in the mid-seventh

---

12 M. Waelkens, et al., "The Late Antique to Early Byzantine city in Southwest Anatolia: Sagalassos and its Territory: A Case Study," in *Die Stadt in der Spätantike: Niedergang oder Wandel?*, ed. Jens-Uwe Krause and Christian Witschel (Stuttgart: Steiner, 2006), 199–255.

century, was, however, believed to have sealed the fate of the urban settlement at Sagalassos.

Yet, even in the earliest articles about these excavations, the excavators knew this was not the complete picture in relation to the overall settlement at Sagalassos. Rural settlement around the site, for example, changed substantially. While villas outside the city walls seem to have dropped off between the fourth and sixth century, farming and agriculture clearly did not. Waelkens points out that much of it was just happening closer to the city walls, probably for protection, and that after the start of the seventh century, village life continued and expanded in the hinterland of Sagalassos, suggesting "a self-sufficient economy centered on villages."[13] This observation is key to understanding the resilience of communities in East Roman archaeology. The shift from the Late Roman world to the medieval period did not see the complete disappearance of the populations, but rather, at Sagalassos, a shift to a more ruralized economy with a local focus. Beyond this, however, the reuse of structures within the city itself provides evidence for understanding the local economies and crafts of the region, including ceramics and metallurgy.

More recent research from Sagalassos has focused both on the reuse of structures in the city, but also on survey of the wider hinterland, which most definitely shows a more rural and localized economy. Much of the evidence for this continuity hinges on a reconsideration of the ceramics at Sagalassos, as well as increased survey in the landscape. In the first instance, the question of ceramics revolves around what the ceramic assemblage looks like in post-Roman Anatolia. Over the last twenty years, the rise in survey projects (as opposed to excavation) has meant that while we have a better understanding of the larger number of medieval sites, we still struggle to date them because these ceramics need to be dated through good stratigraphic excavation. Sagalassos was one of the first sites to be able to provide us with both.

13 Waelkens et al., "The Late Antique," 233, 240.

As noted above, the problem lies with the disappearance of red slip table wares between the seventh and eighth centuries CE. Sagalassos had its own form of this ware, known as Sagalassos Red-Slip Ware, which was locally manufactured and shipped to other parts of Anatolia during the Late Roman period. As with most sites in the Mediterranean, this assemblage was believed to disappear around 700 CE. However, careful consideration of some deposits at Sagalassos now indicates that there is stratigraphic evidence for the continuation of this ware, as well as new dateable ceramics from the seventh through the ninth centuries in what were essentially refuse pits in three former pagan temples. Here the excavators were able to pinpoint specific ceramics which neither conformed to the earlier ceramics nor to later imported glazed ones, which are known from the nearby site known as Alexander's Hill.[14] In doing so the excavators were able to argue that there were five distinct types of ceramics for this period, and a possible lengthier lifespan for locally made red wares than we have traditionally accepted. The continuity of habitation inferred by these observations is really key to a rethinking of what medieval Anatolia looked like, and this corpus has significant ramifications for creating a more precise corpus of ceramics throughout Anatolia using comparative data from other recent excavations like Komana, Amorium, and Çadır Höyük.

Beyond the period from the seventh to ninth centuries, further continuity in the region is illustrated through survey data. While survey work in the earliest reports alludes to potential sites, later work has been able to confirm the presence of small settlements throughout the region.[15] As shown by Talloen et al.,

---

14 Athanasios K. Vionis, Jeroen Poblome, and Marc Waelkens, "The Hidden Material Culture of the Dark Ages. Early Medieval Ceramics at Sagalassos (Turkey): New Evidence (ca. AD 650–800)," *Anatolian Studies* 59 (December 2009): 147–65.

15 Eva Kaptijn et al., "Societal Changes in the Hellenistic, Roman and Early Byzantine Periods: Results from the Sagalassos Territorial Archaeological Survey 2008 (Southwest Turkey)," *Anatolian Studies* 63 (December 2013): 75–95; Ralf Vandam et al., "'Marginal' Landscapes:

the evidence for this is sometimes as simple as the presence of reused stones in the countryside. The widespread scatters of ceramics, now easier to understand with the chronology established in Sagalassos proper, as well as the other material from the survey, provide a much more complete view of the resilience of the region. Indeed, the team at Sagalassos is able to do something unheard of from surface survey in most parts of Anatolia: they can identify sites that had habitation in the early medieval period (seventh-ninth centuries) based on the excavated ceramic data from Sagalassos proper. Further, the nearby town of Ağlasun provides evidence for both a Byzantine church and a Seljuk hammam, which, it has been suggested, may be the location that some of the inhabitants developed as Sagalassos itself became increasingly inhospitable.[16]

The regional analysis of Sagalassos highlights the importance at looking at archaeological material through a regional lens, as well as diachronically. A single site cannot tell us the whole story about how people adapted and changed throughout this period, but understanding the geographical and chronological sequence of this continuity allows us to understand how this population shifted from the Roman world to the medieval one, which can then be compared to other sites. While I have used Sagalassos as the case study here, there are now several other projects working with survey and landscape to illustrate the ways people adapted to changing environments and conditions. For example, Günder Varinlioğlu and her team are tracing settlements throughout Cilicia, with particular focus on the coast regions.[17] The complicated use

---

Human Activity, Vulnerability, and Resilience in the Western Taurus Mountains (Southwest Turkey)," *Journal of Eastern Mediterranean Archaeology and Heritage Studies* 7, no. 4 (November 1, 2019): 432–50; and Peter Talloen et al., "A Byzantine Church Discovered in Aglasan," *Adalya* 20 (2017): 375–404.

16 H. Vanhaverbeke et al., "A Selçuk Hamam at Ağlasun (Burdur Province), Turkey," *Turcica* 37 (2005): 309–36.

17 Günder Varinlioğlu et al., "The 2016 Dana Island Survey: Investigation of an Island Harbor in Ancient Rough Cilicia by the Boğsak

of landscape during the medieval period in the East Roman world is becoming more evident through survey and careful analysis of different artifacts and, in doing this work, we build up a very different picture of medieval Anatolia than we have previously held.

Çadır Höyük[18]

Çadır Höyük serves as a counterpoint to urban settlements like Sagalassos and Assos, and to regional surveys such as that of Rough Cilicia. There is nothing remarkable about the site, other than it is characteristic of rural sites that have been found in many of the Anatolian surveys, such as those of the Cide Project and Project Paphlagonia. That is, it is a small agriculture community that existed throughout the medieval period. To date, it remains one of the only East Roman sites excavated in central Anatolia, and as the ceramic assemblage and dates come into focus, provides an example of a small agricultural community with longstanding continuous habitation. Located in central Anatolia near the modern cities of Sorgun and Yozgat, this was a rural site with evidence for both domestic habitation and small-scale defence in the form of a small walled fortification. While there is minor Roman occupation at the site, the Late Roman and medieval settlements were more robust, occurring both on the mound itself and on the terrace to the north of the mound.

Although a relatively small site, Çadır Höyük exhibits almost continuous habitation from the Chalcolithic period through to the Seljuk settlement in Anatolia. The name of the

Archaeological Survey," *Near Eastern Archaeology* 80, no.1 (March 2017): 50–59; Günder Varinlioğlu, "The Archaeology of Late Antique and Medieval Cilicia: Landscape, Architecture, and Connectivity," *Annuaire de l'École pratique des hautes études: Section des sciences historiques et philologiques* 150 (2019): 188–94.

18 The medieval excavations at Çadır Höyük have been supported in part by funding from the Social Sciences and Humanities Research Council of Canada.

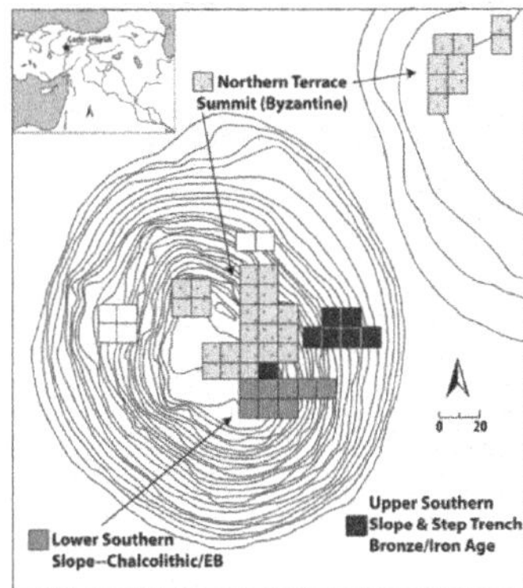

Map 2. Site plan from Çadır Höyük. Courtesy of Çadır Höyük Excavations.

site in antiquity is unknown, and it was almost certainly never a location of major significance in these periods. However, both the domestic and more utilitarian/industrial parts of the site provide evidence for its evolution between the fourth and thirteenth centuries, and this is exemplified by the rebuilding and reuse of structures that is characteristic of East Roman archeology.[19]

The stratigraphic layers at Çadır Höyük offer an unparalleled view of resilience for a medieval population in Anatolia because the site was built and rebuilt so many times, leaving behind a messy but rich stratigraphical legacy. The terrace, which consists of a house which was probably part of a larger village, was built on top of some Imperial Roman remains, confirmed through ^{14}C dates, imported red slip wares, and numismatic evidence. On the mound itself, one small building constructed right on the edge of the mound may have Roman foundations. However, in both cases, the Late Roman period is more visible and clearly identifiable through the material remains, foundations, and related stratigraphy. The Late Roman house on the terrace was of moderate means, and

19 For an introduction to the site, see Marica Cassis, "Çadır Höyük," in Niewöhner, ed., *The Archaeology of Byzantine Anatolia*, 368–75.

Figure 4. Plastered basin from terrace.
Courtesy of Çadır Höyük Excavation.

may have belonged to a local figure of importance, as shown by the presence of imported red slip ware, some luxury items, and plastered surfaces. The house was not fortified, and there is no evidence for extensive defensive structures on either the mound or terrace for this period. The overall impression of the site between the fourth and seventh centuries is that of a moderately prosperous villa or settlement, one with little fear of violence.

As the site transitioned to the medieval period (seventh to ninth centuries), there was a notable downturn in its overall fortunes. While the stratigraphy indicates continuity, the ceramics assemblage gets less and less secure. Like Sagalassos, Çadır Höyük in this period is defined by locally made coarse wares and a declining presence of red slip wares, although there is some attempt in this period to continue manufacturing a local version. Based on ^{14}C dating, the mound seems to be entirely abandoned and unused, in direct contradiction to old wisdom that these mounds were used by panicking "Dark Age" populations. The house on the ter-

Figure 5. Terrace house, original foundations, Late Roman. Flagstone surfaces rebuilt in tenth and eleventh centuries. Courtesy of Çadır Höyük Excavations.

race continued in use, but was reconstructed and subdivided, often with little skill. Yet, the presence of the stratigraphic levels tells us clearly that a population was still there, albeit smaller and perhaps less well-off. This is in keeping with what the environmental data (discussed above) tells us about the region. The pollen samples from Nar Lake, for example, indicate a decline in agricultural crops, and a return of the landscape to weeds and forests. Yet, the population continued to exist in some form.[20]

By the ninth and tenth centuries, more activity returns to the site as a whole. The reconstruction included the addition

20 Marica Cassis et al., "Evaluating Archaeological Evidence for Demographics, Abandonment, and Recovery in Late Antique and Byzantine Anatolia." *Human Ecology : An Interdisciplinary Journal*, 46, no. 3 (2018): 381–98. For the initial Nar Lake data, see England et al., "Historical Landscape Change in Cappadocia (Central Turkey): A Palaeoecological Investigation of Annually Laminated Sediments from Nar Lake," *Holocene (Sevenoaks)* 18, no. 8 (2008): 1229–45.

Figure 6. Storage and food processing rooms on mound at Çadır Höyük. Courtesy of Çadır Höyük Excavations.

of new rooms to the house, including a stable and kitchen area. Parts of the original house were reconstructed with care, and a beautiful flagstone floor is added to some of the older rooms. A plastered courtyard floor appears outside of this structure as well. The mound too now gets a makeover. During the late ninth or early tenth century (based on ^{14}C dates), a well-constructed fortification wall is added to the mound, and the entrance is shifted to the very top of the mound. Guard towers sit along the sides and at the corners of the mound, and the evidence for this period suggests a variety of activities, including metallurgy, agricultural processing (such as grinding grain), and food storage. The mound and the terrace can be seen as two parts of the same community, and it is clear that there was interaction between the two, perhaps with more concentrated help from a local landowner. The construction does not suggest panic, but rather the need to provide continuous moderate security in an agricultural context.

The end of this site came suddenly. In the eleventh century, we see the first real evidence for panic. First, the fortifications were extended, and then some poorly built mud structures were constructed within the walls. At the very end, the gate was blocked. The site fell to invaders in the eleventh century, as witnessed by the abandonment of a large number of animals and the death of some guards. The local population, however, had already fled, probably expecting to return. Although the archaeological evidence suggests that they were not able to do so, the site continued to live on. Sometime in the subsequent hundred years, a Seljuk group, probably herders, used the site both for their animals and as a probable seasonal habitation. They cleared out the east part of the mound, constructed windbreaks on the top, and enacted some rebuilding both on the terrace and mound. Into the Ottoman period, the whole region continued to be used for agricultural purposes, although there is no obvious permanent occupation of the site after about the thirteenth century.

The resilience of the populations who used the site is evident. As with Sagalassos, Çadır Höyük shows a consistent presence throughout the medieval period, one which speaks to the ability of these communities to continue to adapt and evolve as the climate shifted. This was a population that adapted and survived and continued to utilize this agricultural land, albeit on a much smaller scale. While we cannot be sure that the population itself did not change as it probably did with the arrival of the Turks—the consistent use of the site by a population indicates the complexity of site formation and use in the East Roman world. This site was significant enough as an agricultural location to keep being used by a local community. The microhistory of this site can thus be compared to other small sites all over Anatolia in order to understand individual choices that such communities made in terms of where and how they lived. The ability of these communities to adapt over time is an important new direction in our consideration of medieval sites.

Conclusions

Understanding of medieval archaeology has been limited in Anatolia until relatively recently, except in relation to the elite and the religious. This has skewed our understanding of the Late Roman period, and has left large parts of Anatolia out of the discussion completely. Lack of interest coupled with the belief that the seventh century saw the disappearance of many communities was only undone once we began to reconsider the evidence. Sagalassos, Assos, Ephesus, and other cities show how much more complicated the narrative is, and rural excavation and survey, such as that in Rough Cilicia, are now providing opportunities to reconsider continuity and the resilience of rural communities. What is certain, however, is that East Roman medieval archaeology in Anatolia is presenting evidence for resilient communities that adapted to changes in the environment through localized developments. These are vibrant, dynamic communities; increasingly we are questioning how they were connected to one another as well. Understanding this helps us to rethink how regions like Anatolia developed from the Roman world to the medieval world, and subsequently into the early modern one.

Chapter 3

Greece: A Case Study in Landscape Continuity

When my grandmother died, I inherited her large collection of icons. Among my favourites is the icon of St. Phanourios, the patron saint of lost things. My grandmother was a Greek Egyptian, and both of my grandparents were products of the mercantile movement in the Mediterranean during the Ottoman period, their families having originated in Cyprus and perhaps earlier than that, the coast of the Near East. St. Phanourios has become one of my favourite saints for a number of personal reasons—I love his mysterious origins, his connections to Rhodes and Cyprus, the sudden and late rediscovery of his icon (and his story itself) during the Ottoman period, and the movement of his cult throughout the early modern Greek world; his movements parallel my own family history. He is, in himself, a microhistory, one that reflects the complexity of the history of medieval Greece. The layers of the cult of St. Phanourios parallels the complexity of East Roman history and archaeology in medieval Greece, which reflects the same layers of cultural continuity and adaptation to change brought in by new populations. Indeed, perhaps St. Phanourios is looking out for archaeology in Greece, because this archaeology of lost things is really a road map for how we can understand medieval East Roman Greece.

While our understanding of medieval Anatolia remains somewhat limited, Greece offers a more comprehensive view of the *longue durée* of medieval East Roman culture, both because it remains a living, active heritage and simply because more extensive fieldwork has been carried out there, particularly through survey projects. It is to Greece that we can turn to understand the continuity of use of landscapes during the medieval period in both urban and rural settings. Greece had a mixed population, both from invasions and trade, and this is evident in the archaeological record; longevity was fuelled through constant innovation. However, the physical environment, both built and landscape, also provides a backdrop to use and reuse throughout the medieval period. First, excavations in cities like Corinth and Athens provide examples of the kind of site evolution discussed in the previous chapter: the reuse and reinterpretation of space over the medieval period. The extensive data collection from these particular excavations provides nuanced views of the development of material culture and architecture in these urban contexts, as well as the evolution of the cities themselves, precisely because the excavation here has a more robust history than in Türkiye. Second, Greece has had several excellent survey projects which have provided both data and new theoretical insights into the spread of communities in the rural environment, as well as differences between the mainland and island histories. This can be seen in John Bintliff's Boeotia survey, as well as Athanasios Vionis's work in the Cyclades and Fotini Kondyli's work in Lemnos and Thasos in the later medieval period, among others. In all contexts, there can be no doubt that the archaeology of the medieval periods of East Roman Greece provides a case study for understanding change, cultural interaction and borrowing, and adaptation—and above all, longevity.

History of the Field

Initial interest in the archaeology of East Roman Greece did not come about until the early part of the twentieth century, as prior to this the focus at most archaeological sites had only been on the Classical material. Even then, early attention to medieval finds was focused almost exclusively on churches and religious architecture. Nevertheless, unlike in Anatolia, some of the prominent excavations began to preserve and analyze the remains of the Late Roman through medieval periods starting as early as the 1920s and 1930s. As in Türkiye, so in Greece, however, the majority of the early scholarship still concentrated on, particularly, the architectural and monumental remains of the Bronze Age and Classical past. Between the 1830s and the 1880s, almost all of the world powers established research institutes in Greece. Notable among these was the establishment of the American Institute of Archaeology in the 1830s, which eventually led to the excavations in both Corinth and Athens.

Greece's first encounters with the powers of northern Europe presented them with a kind of colonialism that left medieval East Roman archaeology unexplored and at times deliberately removed from archaeological work.[1] Greece has had a complicated relationship with its past, since, although the material culture was of course always there, it was also presented back to the Greeks via the eyes of colonizing Europeans, who saw the Classical world as the foundation not solely of Greek culture but of Europe. Indeed, several authors have argued convincingly that medieval Greece was largely ignored in favour of the Classical past because this idealized past, and not actual convoluted Greek history, had been co-opted into modern European culture.[2] The medieval period—essentially the bridge between the idealized ancient and the European modern—then was seen by others as a corrupted aberration, complete with barbarian conquests and religious, anti-rationalist thought; as such it could be largely

1 Yannis Hamilakis, "Memories Cast in Marble: Introduction," in *The Nation and Its Ruins: Antiquity, Archaeology, and National Imagination in Greece*, ed. by Yannis Hamilakis (Oxford: Oxford University Press, 2007), 1–34; Sofia Voutsaki and Paul Cartledge, eds., *Ancient Monuments and Modern Identities: A Critical History of Archaeology in 19th and 20th Century Greece* (London: Routledge, 2017).

2 Yannis Hamilakis, "Decolonizing Greek Archaeology: Indigenous Archaeologies, Modernist Archaeology and the Post-Colonial Critique," *Μουσείο Μπενάκη*, Supp. 3 (2008): 273–84.

ignored until quite late in the development of Greek archaeology by both Greeks and foreigners.

By the late nineteenth and early twentieth century, however, medieval East Roman history became part of a new form of local nationalism, as it provided a kind of idealized Hellenic, Byzantine identity for the Greek state. The result was the creation of a number of museums and historical sites which celebrated the religious and continuous Hellenic-identity of Greece. This meant that invading cultures such as the Slavs and the Franks were often left out of the narrative.[3] In the early part of the twentieth century, notable figures in the history of church architecture, including Gabrielle Millet, Charles Diehl, and Georges Soteriou, turned their attention to the churches of Greece, which seemed to confirm this narrative. A number of handbooks of art and architecture included Greek churches as well as the icons and frescoes in them. Greece provided good examples of the earliest basilicas, such as those at Philippi, as well as the development of the Greek cross-in-square plan structures known particularly from sites like Hosios Loukas. Paralleling the architectural work was an extensive program of studying the medieval art history of Greece. The monastic context became particularly important for understanding medieval Greece since the records at Mount Athos remain one of the few places that provides a consistent source of documentary evidence. Further, movable art, such as icons, manuscripts, and jewellery became representative of the East Roman revival between the ninth and eleventh centuries. In short, the combination of the artistic and written evidence traditionally focused the attention of scholars of material culture on religious and elite East Roman society. It is only through archaeology that this narrative has changed.

---

3 Bintliff, *Complete Archaeology of Greece*, 382–83.

Urban Continuity

Increased interest in the lives of East Roman communities started in the urban excavations at Corinth and Athens. In order to illustrate this, I will focus here on Corinth, as the recent work of Guy Sanders is formative in the way urban sites are now being reconsidered. As well, it offers an important case study in both the way the approach of archaeologists to medieval archaeology has changed, and to the documented continuity of site usage. Excavations at Corinth began in the 1920s, and stemmed from what Kourelis has argued was an off-shoot of the *avant-garde* culture of the 1920s, a culture which saw the Byzantine as exotic and in some ways subversive, precisely because it was not the much-valued Classical world.[4] While the earliest excavations at Corinth were not always of the highest quality, enough information was collected to create a narrative on the chronology of medieval Corinth, material which was to form the basis of later discussions of material culture from the site, including, significantly, the coins and ceramics.[5] The care for the medieval was quite unusual among excavators; nevertheless it remained until the 1950s and 1960s for real scholarly analysis of Late Roman and medieval Corinth to begin.

While it is beyond the scope of this work to dissect the excavations at Corinth in detail, there are two important points in relation to this site that illustrate the continuity of use of East Roman sites. First, as with most medieval sites in the East Roman world, the earliest assumptions were based on the idea of decline and abandonment. These assumptions were based on the findings noted in the earliest archaeological reports in which the lack of ceramics and coinage from

---

4 Kostis Kourelis, "Byzantium and the Avant-Garde: Excavations at Corinth, 1920s-1930s," *Hesperia* 76 no. 2 (August 7, 2007): 391–442.

5 Guy Sanders, "Recent Developments in the Chronology of Byzantine Corinth" in *Corinth: The Centenary: 1896–1996* (Princeton: American School of Classical Studies at Athens, 2003), 385–99.

the seventh to ninth centuries seemed to suggest a complete break between the Late Roman and the later medieval periods. This was combined with the lack of mention of most Greek sites in the contemporary primary sources, which, in more general terms, often present the period as one of catastrophe and decline, largely through a religious lens. In fact, as will be illustrated below, a redating and reconsideration of parts of the site actually show remarkable continuity of habitation. Connected to this is a second point of caution. As identified by Sanders, the former director of the excavations at Corinth, characteristics of East Roman urban settlements cannot be universally applied to other cities across the board, nor to the rural hinterlands that surround them. That is, Sanders indicates that each site needs to be understood with independent research questions that separate urban and rural communities, and see each site as reflective of its own social and environmental factors.[6] This too is an important current and evolving area of research which speaks again to the importance of the microhistorical approach.

The first problem goes back to the assumption that Greek sites underwent the same abandonment that we saw applied to Anatolian ones, which Sanders identifies as "the spasmodic cycle of prosperity followed by catastrophe culminating in complete collapse."[7] As we have seen, this concept was applied to most urban settlements all over the Eastern medieval world, both as a way of explaining the importance of particular environmental and social events visible in the written sources, such as earthquakes and invasions, and as a way of explaining periods where the artifacts of daily life become difficult to trace. The problem is that this is not how human societies function; events affecting a site tend to happen over a longer process, with changes to the built environment effected based on human reactions and adaptations to events as (and after) they happen. Even

6 Sanders, "Problems in Interpreting Rural and Urban Settlement in Southern Greece, AD 365–700," in *Landscapes of Change*, 163–93.

7 Sanders, "Problems," 169.

when events are sudden and catastrophic, the resultant changes can be slow and adaptive. This is why the resilience theory discussed in relation to Anatolia is so significant. It moves us away from the idea of cause and effect, to one where we can see how societies, just like any other part of the natural world, adapt.

In the example of Corinth, for example, we move from a period of growth at the end of the Imperial Roman period around the fourth century, to one of conservation. What does this term mean, in archaeological context? Following the ideas presented in the last chapter, this is a period where the local environment is retained and reused by those who can, but it is not a period of growth. In the case of Corinth, over the fifth and sixth centuries buildings were subdivided and reused, and parts of the city were walled off or excluded and adapted for different use, possibly in reaction to earthquake damage. In Corinth, the Forum, for example, became a place for graves starting in the fifth century, and remained in use until about the eighth century.[8] While the Late Roman period at Corinth is still marked by the ability to clearly date stratigraphy through the use of ceramics and coinage, it leads directly into the medieval, or what we would think of as a period of release, whereby there is even less infrastructure and organization in the urban centre, and people seem to move into other areas outside the city. This is quite often the period associated with complete abandonment. This change can be loosely connected to the period of the seventh to the early ninth century, where a combination of major factors (like earthquakes and invasions) occurred within the overall societal and environmental changes that were endemic in this period. In the ninth century, another earthquake hit the town, doing massive damage and killing thousands. But a key point is that there *were* people still living there, something clearly indicated by the stratigraphical excavations. The reorganization, then, comes in the ninth century, when restructuring and rebuilding took place throughout the East Roman world,

8 Sanders, "Problems," 176–81.

a result, again, of both social and environmental changes, since this marked a period of less disruption.

In effect, what Sanders was able to show through the reconsideration of stratigraphic evidence was that the boom/bust cycle was neither provable nor likely at Corinth. Rather, what *was* visible was adaptation of a society to the social and environmental changes which began in the fifth century. The cyclical nature of societal change is far less abrupt than the extreme ideas of destruction and abandonment that have been traditionally accepted. This is most evident, for example, in ceramics analysis, where we see the slow phasing out of imported fine wares during the sixth century, which was generally assumed to have happened because of disruptions to production and trade. It is only possible to transport such goods when roads and other travel routes are strong and protected; the wider infrastructure has to remain in place. Thus, the disappearance of imported ceramics did not happen overnight, and of course there were legacy artifacts that continued in use. However, as it became increasingly difficult to transport fine wares, there was a resulting reliance on locally made coarse wares. The same is true of coinage, which largely disappeared in the seventh century, a result of a shift to more local economies. These changes do not, however, reflect the destruction of an entire society.

Stratigraphical analysis, then, shows that life did continue, although only recently have the dates become clearer. This has largely been accomplished through reconsiderations of coarse wares and site reuse, such as graves. Indeed, Sanders argues against the overuse of fine wares and coins as points of dating, when the rest of the evidence, most notably coarse wares, has been largely ignored or underrepresented.[9] One of the other things that was expected of most of Greece, for example, was the presence of ceramics which reflected the arrival of the Slavs in the seventh century. While there are some (although there are many debates about these), Bintliff

9 Sanders, "Recent Developments," 394.

points out that the lack of large numbers of ceramics for the Slavic invasions of much of Greece in the seventh century are not visible in the pottery record because the populations largely integrated with one another.[10] Nevertheless, reconsidering these coarse wares, as scholars like Sanders, Pamela Armstrong, and Joanita Vroom have done for Greece, helps to fill this gap in our understanding of the early medieval period, where the old ways gave way to new organizational structures which reflect more localized traditions.

It is worth pointing out that Corinth is not an anomaly in terms of continuous urban usage and adaptation. Similar patterns of habitation can be located in the Agora in Athens, where the American School has been excavating Late Roman and medieval material since approximately the same time as Corinth. Indeed, Alison Frantz was pivotal in analyzing this material and tracing the importance of medieval Athens.[11] As Fotini Kondyli has shown, although there is much more work to be done, continuity of use can be traced from the Late Roman period through the Early Byzantine period, into the Middle Byzantine period.[12] Using this data as a starting point, she asks new questions about how neighbourhoods were organized and the way structures were used and reused within these medieval contexts. Similarly, the excavations in the Agora have allowed for new discussions of ceramics assemblages. Frantz began this with her careful consideration of the fine wares particularly, and more recently Joanita Vroom has begun to reconsider ceramics types from particularly the seventh through ninth centuries. Her analysis is significant because she is already showing that the continuity in the transitional period from the Late Roman to the early medieval is more well-attested than has previously been thought, primarily through the use of ceramics specific to

10 Bintliff, *Complete Archaeology of Greece*, 384–85.

11 Alison Frantz, *The Middle Ages in the Athenian Agora* (Princeton: American School of Classical Studies at Athens, 1961).

12 Kondyli, "The View from Byzantine Archaeology," in *The Byzantine Neighbourhood*, 44–69.

this period.[13] This in turn can be considered alongside the evidence form Corinth.

Rural Continuity

As noted elsewhere, the idea of decline started in relation to the urban context, but moved to encompass rural settlements as well. However, if we can now agree that continuity looked different in an urban context than we expected, then it becomes possible to also see that in relation to the individual rural contexts. In large part, early focus in East Roman studies was primarily on the urban centres, which is a holdover from previous studies of the Roman world, again because medieval archaeology grew out of Classical archaeology. So, rural sites, which are not impressive and are largely invisible, were rarely a topic of discussion until relatively recently, unless they contained obvious fortifications or churches. The lack of data helped confirm the idea that societies simply stopped functioning between the seventh and ninth century. Yet, anyone who has ever walked through villages in Greece or Anatolia knows that there is plenty of evidence in the countryside for continuous life: reused columns in graves, architectural blocks built into churches, mosques, or houses, copious ceramics in agricultural fields, and early monumental architecture reused as utilitarian structures.

Recent surveys of Greece have proven that there is a much more consistent and comprehensive life for sites in the countryside than we have considered. The problem with survey is that it often provides data that spans a vast time period, and for the medieval period, the coarse ware is notoriously difficult to date. As pottery sequences have improved in Greece, however, it is possible to see the continuity of medieval land use in these survey results, a point made by the

13 Joanita Vroom, "Byzantine Butrint Vis-à-Vis 'Dark Age' Athens: A Ceramic Perspective" in *Byzantine Greece: Microcosm of Empire?*, ed. Brian McLaughlin and Archibald Dunn (Abingdon: Routledge, 2023), 166–81.

Figure 7. Syriac Church reused as stable in the Tur Abdin.

surveys around Corinth and in Boeotia.[14] An examination of the results from both shows communities that continued (and at times expanded) in the Late Roman period, and contracted in the medieval period (between the seventh and ninth centuries) but did not disappear. Rather, as the environment and society changed, these populations adapted to the social and environmental changes in very specific ways, creating small villages and settlements. It is precisely these small settlements that archaeologists are turning their attention to in order to fully understand medieval Greece.

The most prominent of these surveys is undoubtedly Bintliff's extensive survey of Boeotia.[15]

---

14 John Bintliff, "Central Greece in Late Antiquity: The Evidence from the Boeotia Project" in *Field Methods and Post-Excavation Techniques in Late Antique Archaeology*, ed. Luke Lavan and Michael Mulryan (Leiden: Brill, 2015), 187–203.

15 J. L. Bintliff, et al., *Testing the Hinterland: The Work of the Boeotia*

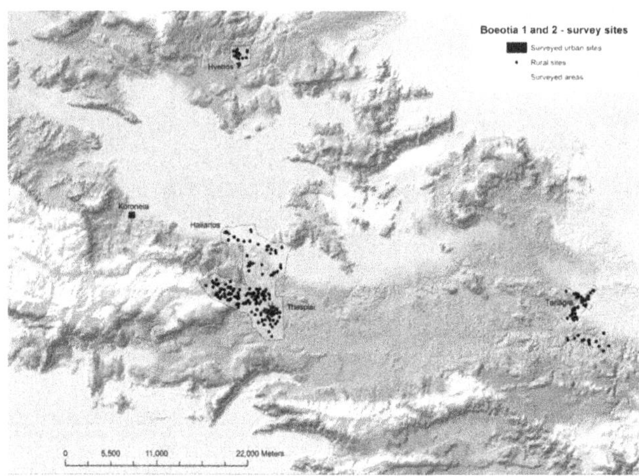

Map 3. Map of identified sites, Boeotia Survey project. From https://www.boeotiaproject.org/, July 10, 2024. Used with permission.

Bintliff's work is significant because he recognized that earlier regional surveys struggled with identifying non-monumental East Roman features and material culture in the landscape, most notably ceramics. In part this was because he also recognized that the team was missing cultural markers for the prehistoric period as well. With time, Bintliff's team recognized that this was not because they were not there, but that the numbers of sherds for small prehistoric settlements were often difficult to identify, due to intense reuse of lands, agricultural techniques during the Classical period, and the overall wear and tear on any early sherds that did make it to the surface. Similarly, for the medieval periods, ceramics and sites were difficult to identify, because the primary sources suggested the surveyors should be looking for specific cultural markers. This meant searching for very specific markers

Survey (1989–1991) in the Southern Approaches to the City of Thespiai (Cambridge: Mcdonald Institute of Archaeological Research, 2007).

that did not exist, like the so-called Slavic wares that were supposed to represent invasion.

As noted several times, the coarse wares for the medieval period are difficult to analyze, and this meant that, given the lack of fine wares, it was easy in earlier reports to underestimate the number of medieval villages. By thinking about the importance of geography, Bintliff was able to see medieval communities as shifting with specific landscapes, but still remaining present, as visible through the large but scattered numbers of numbers of these coarse wares. Bintliff's survey analysis shows, in fact, that it was geography and landscape use which played a huge part in the continuity of communities in medieval Boeotia, and was in fact the driving force in integrating different ethnicities and groups into the region. Importantly, however, these were often small, short-lived communities, and did not mark cultural continuity as much as geographical continuity, a point that helps to dispel the idea of a uniform Hellenic culture.[16]

This concept of geographical continuity and land use is key to also understanding the social contexts of late East Roman communities, where a lot more written and archaeological evidence exists. These projects provide evidence for complicated, interconnected, and complex rural villages in the Late Medieval (and post-medieval) period and provide a model for understanding how such villages functioned and adapted.[17] Sharon Gerstel's work on Late Medieval Greece uses ethnographic, archaeological and art historical evidence to illustrate a possible way of understanding the "overlapping landscapes: agricultural, domestic, and sacred" of late

16 John Bintliff et al., "Deconstructing 'The Sense of Place'? Settlement Systems, Field Survey, and the Historic Record: A Case-Study from Central Greece," *Proceedings of the Prehistoric Society* 66 (2000): 123–49.

17 Sanders, "Landscape," 187 says "survey must realise that later periods, especially the early modern, for which there is a rich textual, monumental and ethnographic record, offer much scope for understanding more ancient landscapes."

medieval Greece.[18] The quantity of information for this period allows us to envision the past more completely, and to understand possible ways villages functioned. Fotini Kondyli, on the other hand, explicitly uses resilience theory to look at networks of villages and homes through the island populations of Thasos and Lemnos in the late medieval period, illustrating a dense and complex network of villages.[19] Her work, which combines the archaeological survey and written evidence shows a continuous use of landscape over the later medieval period, confirming our understanding of resilience in the medieval period. Finally, both ethnographic and archaeological research show the continuity of land use in the Cyclades in Athanasios Vionis's survey results.[20] Importantly, the work in the islands also shows microregional differences from the mainland. This is a new direction that needs further work, as the islands dealt with different landscapes, different environmental challenges, and often, different cultural interactions with outsiders, a point discussed in chapter five in relation to Cyprus and Sicily. Simply by recognizing variation, and reconsidering archaeological markers, new evidence and new questions appear.

Conclusions

Byzantine archaeology in Greece has developed consistently since first explorations in the 1920s and 1930s. The urban sites show clear examples of continuous reuse and rebuilding, and excavation now provides enough data to move towards better social analysis of communities, as in the work of Kondyli and Bintliff. Rural sites in Greece are now better identified in survey, but, as in Anatolia, require more exca-

---

18 Gerstel, *Rural Lives and Landscapes in Late Byzantium*, 4.

19 Kondyli, *Rural Communities in Late Byzantium*.

20 Athanasios K. Vionis, "Domestic Material Culture and Post-Medieval Archaeology in Greece: A Case-Study from the Cyclades Islands," *Post-Medieval Archaeology* 39, no. 1 (March 2005): 172–85.

vation. Nevertheless, the intense surveys such as that of the Boeotia Project provide an important view of the interconnection between landscape and community in creating continuity. Rather than hinging such data to written sources, expected outcomes, or general decline, rural landscapes now clearly indicate that it is geography and landscape which drives community building, and which often allowed for the integration of new communities that entered Greece, such as the Slavs and the Franks. It is in Greece that we have the most comprehensive ceramics analysis, and this data shows that Greek villages and urban environments moved through cycles of resilience and reorganization which speak to continuity. This then adds to the model that can be considered for other parts of the medieval world. Each village, each town in Greece provides another microhistorical entrance into the East Roman world.

Chapter 4

The Levant: A Case Study in Identities

Of all the art, architecture, and archaeology in the Near East, there is one structure that always strikes me as symbolic of the layers of history in the region: the Dome of the Rock in Jerusalem. Constructed in the early Umayyad period, it is situated over the former site of the Jewish Temple in the Haram al-Sharif. It was built to commemorate Muhammad's Night Journey and its central feature is the stone from which he is believed to have ascended to heaven. It is, of course, an important Islamic monument, and much has been written about the construction, rebuildings, and purpose of the structure. Nevertheless, what always strikes me as significant about it is the evidence it contains for cultural borrowing in the seventh century. The inscriptions are in Arabic but are aimed at non-Muslims; the rotunda shape has its roots in Late Roman architecture. Textual evidence tells us that the East Roman emperor sent materials and craftsmen to help decorate the structure, which is filled with beautiful non-figural mosaics, and these images, many of them jewelled vegetal motifs, represent both East Roman and Sasanian artistic traditions.[1] In so many ways the Dome of the Rock is symbolic of the rich mixed heritage of the region.

---

1 For complete discussion, see Oleg Grabar, *The Dome of the Rock* (Cambridge: Belknap, 2006). For an important discussion of cultural and artistic borrowing of Sasanian motifs in the East Roman world, see Matthew P. Canepa, *The Two Eyes of the Earth: Art and Ritual of*

This interconnected history in the Levant is pivotal in any consideration of East Roman archaeology, but in some ways it is also the most problematic. Much of the archaeology in this region which includes modern Israel, Palestine, Jordan, Lebanon, and Syria has traditionally been seen as *either* East Roman (Byzantine is almost always the term used in the region, reflecting imperial control until the arrival of the Muslims) or Islamic. The East Roman period ends in the mid-seventh century with the arrival of the Arab Muslims, at which point archaeology in the region largely becomes identified as Islamic archaeology, as a way of distinguishing it from what came before. Christian archaeology remains just that, and is separated by its religious nature. East Roman archaeology in the Levant, then, only refers to Late Roman material and has historically been concerned with Christian religious architecture and art. During the late nineteenth and early twentieth centuries, archaeology was largely a religious archaeology of Christianity in the Holy Land, with explicit connections to Christianity in Europe. Islamic archaeology, on the other hand, was originally seen by colonizing Europeans and scholars in a relatively negative light, and indicative of the downturn in fortunes in the region.

Three important changes to both of these disciplines over the last thirty years have started to bring them closer together. First, there has been increased research into small villages and farming centres and the non-monumental nature of this archaeology negates the earlier clear division between the two periods. Scholars have tried to address this by using more inclusive language, identifying sites by the period of specific caliphates (Umayyad archaeology, for example). Second, many scholars have rethought the historical and religious evidence that suggests that the arrival of the Arabs resulted in the decline of the region.[2] More careful reading of the archaeological evidence indicates that there was, in

Kingship Between Rome and Sasanian Iran (Berkeley: University of California Press, 2009).

2 For a good introduction to the history of the literature, see Jodi

fact, considerable evidence for continuity in habitation from the seventh through tenth centuries in some areas, and that most of it cannot be clearly linked only to religious affiliations. Finally, work in the liminal zones of the Levant on the borders between empires is helping to address interactions among ordinary people during the East Roman/Islamic periods. The archaeology of the Levant thus becomes a place where the term medieval becomes more important as it breaks down the barriers between groups that must have continued to live alongside one another, at times sharing artistic and architectural techniques and imagery. I would argue that holding on to the old divisions does not help us understand how the region evolved with the arrival of the Muslims, and keeps us from fully understanding the interaction and integration of these communities.

History of the Field

There are three strands to the development of a Late Roman and medieval archaeology in the Levant. First, there was an early fascination with Jerusalem and Palestine, starting in the mid- to late nineteenth century, which played on the European obsession with the history of the Bible. This was the same impetus which sent early explorers into Mesopotamia looking for the remains of the Old Testament. Biblical archaeology was a real driving factor in the initial European exploration of holy sites throughout the region. By the end of the nineteenth and into the early twentieth centuries, more serious scholarship was being carried out by scholars attempting to record the remains of Christian churches throughout the region. Finally, in the early part of the twentieth century, excavations of explicitly Christian and/or medieval structures were undertaken. The one thing that connected all three of these phases of development was the fascination with the land as indicative of a primitive Christianity which could

Magness, *The Archaeology of Early Islamic Settlement in Palestine*, 195–214.

explain and elucidate European Christianity. This too was a form of colonialism, although it was explicitly religious in nature, and was a way for Europeans to explore what they perceived as their own heritage.[3]

Among the most significant figures in the first two phases were scholars who attempted to detail and record many of the earliest churches in the Levant. Among the first, for example, was Charles-Jean-Melchior de Vogüe, who carefully detailed many churches in the Holy Land.[4] He was followed by prominent scholars like Charles Butler and Earl Baldwin Smith, who did the same for Syria under the auspices of Princeton and the American Archaeological Expedition to Syria.[5] By the early part of the twentieth century, a number of different sites were being scientifically excavated, although, as noted above, the focus was almost entirely on the period between Constantine and the rise of Islam, and most of the work was designed to record early churches and monasteries. This work included sites in places like Antioch (Charles Morey and Glanville Downey); Apameia (Fernand Mayence and Jean Charles Balty); and Gerasa (John Crowfoot and Carl Kraeling). This is in no way a comprehensive list of the work, which was already intense in the region in the early part of the twentieth century. There were also other kinds of scientific work being carried out, such as surveys and mapping exercises by figures like Charles Clermont-Ganneau in Palestine and, perhaps most notably, Georges Tchalenko, who surveyed the villages and churches of the so-called Dead Cities of Syria.[6]

---

3 William Caraher and David Pettegrew, "The Archaeology of Early Christianity," in *The Oxford Handbook of Early Christian Archaeology*, 1–27. The chapters on the various regions of the Levant in this book also provide good insight into the wider issues in the field.

4 Charles Jean Melchior Vogue, *Les églises de la Terre Sainte* (Paris: Didion, 1860).

5 Butler, *Early Churches in Syria*.

6 Georges Tchalenko, *Églises de village de la Syrie du Nord* (Paris: Geuthner, 1979) and Georges Tchalenko, *Villages antiques de la Syrie du Nord: Le massif du Bélus à l'époque romaine* (Paris: Geuthner, 1953).

Much of the work in the early part of the twentieth century also had military overtones. It was out of such explorations that remarkable finds were made at places like Palmyra and Dura Europos, where both the earliest extant church and one of the earliest synagogues were discovered.

As we saw with Türkiye, many of these early scholarly works remain an invaluable source of information, particularly for churches and other structures that are no longer extant. The problem of course is that much of this work was again focused almost exclusively on monumental architecture and standing remains, and while this provided a great deal of information about the development of the architecture of the early church, it did little to illustrate the continuity among communities or indeed the ordinary village lives of the populations in the region. Early excavations, as elsewhere, often did little to conserve the remains of the medieval past, although the long-term nature of excavations in the Levant means that more remains and more records are extant, and slowly but surely people are returning to these documentary accounts.

Overall, one of the biggest problems with the earliest work is that it defined people entirely by religious belief, which implies static identities. By default, then, as the term Byzantine was more commonly used, it also simply became shorthand for Christian, suggesting that these populations were largely unimportant during what became the Islamic period. The arrival of the Crusaders brought a whole new type of Christian material culture, and their presence completely overshadowed the Christians who had been in the region for centuries. The term "Byzantine" also lumped all Christians together as one group, which resulted in the loss of identity for the many different groups that lived and developed in the Levant in this period, including the Melkites, Maronites, West Syriac, and Armenian Christians. I will address the problems of identity surrounding local Christianities in the final chapter. For our purposes, here, the problem lies in the static image we accept when we rely solely on religious identity and terminology to define communities. The reality was much more complex, as the next section will show.

Rethinking Villages and Communities

There are two aspects to the current reconsideration of Levantine villages and communities (including cities) in archaeological work. The first revolves around the impact of Islam on East Roman communities in the mid-seventh century. It is important to stress that many populations did not cease to exist, or indeed even change substantially, with the arrival of Islam. The second aspect focuses on whether we can see multiple identities in the extant evidence without relying entirely on religious architecture. That is, what is the role of domestic and secular architecture in community building and identity? Here it becomes important to think about how these communities borrowed from one another.

For the Levant, and in particular from Israel and Palestine, there is an embarrassment of riches for illustrating major historical shifts as there has been such a large amount of excavation and survey in these regions. While in Greece and Anatolia, the question focuses on decline in the sixth century, for the Levant the focus is on the impact of the Islamic invasions on the local populations. Inherent in the division between Byzantine and Islamic as categories is the notion that there was an overwhelming change to society. The implication is also that it was necessarily negative, which seems to be supported by the primary sources from the period immediately after the advent of Islam which suggest that this was an apocalyptic event, and perhaps even punishment from God. The reality, however, is of course much more complex than this, and recent archaeological work by scholars such as Gideon Avni, Jodi Magness, and Ken Dark indicates that there is little evidence that the arrival of Islam caused any major breakdown of society as a whole.[7] In fact, once again, we return to the concept of the microhistory, which shows that there cannot be a single answer for the entire region. Furthermore, most identifiable changes occurred long

---

7 Avni, *The Byzantine-Islamic Transition in Palestine*, particularly 191–299 and Ken Dark, *Roman-Period and Byzantine Nazareth and its Hinterland* (London: Routledge, 2020).

after the arrival of Islam, and often for environmental reasons linked to changing climate or natural disasters.

Three prominent examples illustrate the complexity of understanding the evolution of the villages in these regions. In his work on Palestine, Avni was able to locate both Jewish and Christian villages which show consistent development into the eighth and ninth century; no major break occurred in the seventh century. This argument is largely based on the continued ceramics typologies and agricultural field use as established through survey data. He stresses however, that the results are different in different places. As a case study, he looks at two areas of the Negev. In the eastern Negev, settlements declined in the eighth century, while in the western section, they continued as late as the tenth century.[8] Dark illustrates that there is evidence for the decline of the area around Nazareth by the end of the seventh century, but that the pilgrimage centre and city remained strongly inhabited.[9] Thus, there cannot have been a major disruption to Christian villages, but rather this appears to have been a complicated set of reactions to situational events such as earthquakes. Thus, while while at first glance the archaeological data seems to equate the arrival of Islam with the decline of the region, the continuation of the religious site makes this unlikely. Instead, understanding the whole picture of these regions provides a different view of how communities adapted to any number of changes.

A third important example is connected to the dates for the so-called Dead Cities in Syria, as exemplified by the site of Dehes.[10] Jodi Magness re-examined the archaeological evi-

---

8 Avni, *The Byzantine-Islamic Transition in Palestine*, 287.

9 Dark, *Roman-Period and Byzantine Nazareth*, 148–50.

10 Magness, *The Archaeology of Early Islamic Settlement*, 205–6 and Walmsley, *Early Islamic Syria: An Archaeological Assessment*, 23–28. The original excavations were by Jean-Pierre Sodini et al., "Déhès (Syrie du nord): Campagnes I–III (1976–1978). Recherches sur l'habitat rural," *Syria* 57, no. 1 (1980): 1–304.

Figure 8. West Church, Dehes. Dumbarton Oaks Research Library and Collection, PHBZ024_2016_4521. Photograph by Frank Kidner. CC-BY-SA 4.0.

dence from the excavations carried out at the site of Dehes subsequent to Tchalenko's survey in order to look at the varying theories about the decline of the site. Tchalenko's work suggested an abandonment with the arrival of Islam in the region (largely based on the disappearance of epigraphic evidence), while others such as Sodini argued for an earlier decline in the sixth century, with a subsequent abandonment. Magness's re-examination of the evidence shows with with certainty that the ceramics date to at least the sixth century, and based on the redating of many red wares later than the start of the seventh century, she has shown that Dehes continued to be inhabited later than the arrival of the Muslims. Indeed, there is evidence for continued habitation through to the ninth or tenth century, information which can be extrapolated to many of the other villages of the region. In fact, the material culture and ceramics are in direct contradiction to the earlier concerns about the lack of epigraphy. Some of the buildings were constructed *after* the buildings with inscriptions, and the villages continued in use for a long time after the construction of late sixth and seventh century buildings. Her re-examination of the archaeological evidence is a good example of the importance of returning to earlier archaeological material to reconsider what we think we know. Magness has made the same kinds of arguments for Antioch, which is supported by evidence for the continuation of the use of many of the churches in the city.[11] In short, we must be careful to not connect historical events with archaeological evidence if it does not support the link.

If sites continued in use throughout the eighth and ninth centuries (at least), what then can we say about identity? There can be no doubt that some sites continued to be specifically Christian or Jewish, and that others were settled by Muslims. However, the majority of evidence suggests that it is simply not possible to identify religious affiliation in the remaining archaeological material. Magness, for example, indicates that there is little evidence for it at Dehes, and Dark shows that the Jewish community in Nazareth continued to function there, alongside Christians and Muslims. Nor does there appear to be any kind of wide-scale conversion, at least not enough to disrupt the majority of pilgrimage sites, such as that at Nazareth, as we have seen. In short, it seems as if many communities in the Levant continued as they always had, and that eventual decline came as a result of community reactions to primarily environmental factors, as in the Negev. This is not mean to downplay the written evidence or the significance of understanding religious structures. But the evidence from the Levant is not as clear cut as we have traditionally assumed it to be.

To this conversation we can also add the situation surrounding travel, both for religious devotion and for trade. Both Avni and Dark draw attention to the presence of trade networks in their respective regions, and is clear that some of this trade was between different religious communities. More telling, however, is the evidence for religious travel. First,

11 For Antioch, U. de Giorgi and A. Asa Eger, *Antioch: A History* (Milton: Taylor and Francis, 2021), 235–76.

monastic and pilgrimage sites which were established in the Late Roman period continue unabated into the early Islamic period, and some in fact expand their influence. Avni and Dark have found evidence for this in several locations in Jordan and Palestine, and, as noted, De Giorgi and Eger draw attention to the continuation of several churches in Antioch. Continuous devotion at Bethlehem and Jerusalem continues as well.

Secondly, some sites begin to show remarkable connections between believers of different faiths, particularly those sites with connections to the Old Testament. Here I would draw your attention to the excavations of the church and chapel at Petra on the Mountain of Aaron, excavated by Fiema and Frösén.[12] These excavations carefully traced this site through the Byzantine, Islamic, and crusader periods, and while there were different forms of devotion from Muslims and Christians, the site remained important to all throughout the medieval period. While the site is particularly useful for understanding the evolution of the church structure, the continuity is remarkable, as is the fact that the site itself was considered sacred to Muslim communities by the late medieval period.

A final example comes from the monastic churches in modern Jordan. These structures are well-known for their pilgrimage and monastic functions. More than that, however, they give us a look into the identities of the communities who used them in the medieval period. As with the dates for the decline of Christian communities in Palestine, changes within these structures have often been connected with the arrival of the Muslims. This is largely because many of the mosaic floors in these structures had figural imagery removed over the course of their use. However, close examination of these changes suggests that they may have been primarily internally motivated, reflecting liturgical and religious changes in the church between the fifth and eighth centuries.

---

12 Zbigniew T. Fiema, et al., *Petra—The Mountain of Aaron: The Church and the Chapel*, The Finnish Archaeological Project in Jordan (Helsinki: Societas Scientiarum Fennica, 2008).

Figure 9. Excavated monastery at Jabal Harun. https://commons.wikimedia.org/wiki/File:Byzantine_church_ruins_near_Mt._Aaron_2008-09-27.jpg. Photograph by Joneikifi. CC-BY-SA 4.0.

First, an early change in some of the churches in the pre-Islamic period involves the consecration of permanent altars in the secondary phase of the church development. This can be seen in several churches, such as the Chapel of the Priest John at Khirbat al-Mukhayyat, and at the Church of the Deacon Thomas at 'Uyun Musa.[13] Both churches were built in the late fifth or early sixth century, and then during the mid-sixth century, both churches had a permanent altar added to the sanctuary area, marring the original images of the mosaic. This kind of change to the church suggests important changes in liturgical structures, ones that I have elsewhere connected to the move to a more standardized Late Roman liturgy under Justinian. A second example occurs in a couple of the churches of Madaba, such as the Church of the Bishop Sergius, and the original structure dates to the sixth century. Here, at some point after that, the floors were carefully reorganized to remove all figural imagery. This was done through a reorganization of mosaic tesserae to neatly

---

13 Anne Michel, *Les églises d'époque byzantine et umayyade de Jordanie (provinces d'Arabie et de Palestine) V[e] -VIIe siècle: Typologie architecturale et aménagements liturgiques (avec catalogue des monuments)* (Turnhout: Brepols: 2001).

Figure 10. Mosaic from the Church of the Deacon Thomas at 'Uyun Musa. Courtesy of the Franciscan Custody of the Holy Land, Mt. Nebo, and the American Center of Research, Amman.

but deliberately remove images of living beings. Although this kind of change had traditionally been associated with the arrival of the aniconic Muslims, it is now widely accepted by scholars that this may have been a result of internal religious beliefs or even iconoclast tendencies in the eighth century, as the change was never consistent. Here, internal identity markers of small monastic communities need to be seen as such, rather than being applied to these communities based on an external motivation with no evidence.

Rethinking Borders

To end this section, I would draw attention to particularly important new work that is happening in the liminal or border zones between the East Roman and Islamic worlds, where we can specifically consider the kind of interactions that happened between groups, and whether this had any effect on group identity. This is hard material to classify because it transcends geographical and cultural boundaries. Once again, the arrival of Islam in the region, followed by notable skirmishes across that border in both the Umayyad and Abbasid periods, led to a fairly strict idea of the differentiation between communities. Certainly, both the historical and religious texts tell us this, and there is no doubt that at times this was more intense than others. However, this cannot be the whole story. For example, around the start of the ninth century, there was little in the way of raids on Anatolia as the new Islamic caliphate reorganized itself.

Asa Eger has led the scholarship on this material, resulting in reconsideration of what these border areas actually looked like. Indeed, his survey work has conclusively shown that the so-called no man's land between Syria and what is today Türkiye was nowhere near as abandoned as we had previously believed.[14] Indeed, multiple settlements and towns, as well as a vibrant trade network, functioned between the two areas, creating much more interaction between the communities than the historical narrative would have us believe. This work has led to further consideration of this type of daily interaction, particularly in relation to border cities like Antioch, as well as other liminal zones. This provides a model for thinking further about contacts between Christians and Muslims, about trade routes, and about the transference of technologies and ideas between communities.[15] It opens up new questions that might help us understand how goods and knowledge moved across community boundaries.

14 Eger, *The Islamic-Byzantine Frontier*.

15 For an interesting examination of this in relation to Palestine, see Hagit Nol, *Settlement and Urbanization in Early Islamic Palestine* (Abingdon: Routledge, 2022).

Conclusions

While there is not space in a book of this size to get into all of the nuances of this problem, I would suggest that the labels traditionally used in the Levant have created false dichotomies between medieval populations when geographical locations (microregions) would be far more useful. I have concentrated here on the transition from the Late Roman to the early Islamic period because there is much that is new in this area. The most recent scholarship has been very clear that much of the data needs to be reconsidered in order to see a more nuanced understanding of how people representing multiple identities lived together and, at times, shared technologies and religious structures. By continuing to place these groups into their own religious categories, we forget that they all lived together (whether peacefully or not) and moved material culture across borders (formally or not). Indeed, the medieval period saw people express multiple identities based on the town or village they lived in, the religion they espoused, the language they spoke, and the people they engaged with. This is what the Levant offers us: a place to see the medieval world as complicated, messy, and a model for understanding other, less documented parts of the Near East.

Chapter 5

Including the Other: Local and Liminal Communities

In 2019, I was invited to join a group of scholars assessing Syriac remains in the Tur Abdin in eastern Türkiye for the *Kültürel Mirası Koruma Derneği* (Association for the Protection of Cultural Heritage). This trip was pivotal in my approach to the East Roman world, because, although I had studied these churches for many years, it was only on seeing them and walking through the undocumented villages and cemeteries surrounding them, that I came to understand how much we are actually missing in terms of our understanding of the medieval East Roman world by siloing localized and liminal communities from what has traditionally been termed "Byzantine" archaeology. These particular communities in eastern Türkiye drew from so many disparate places, from the imperial Roman world, from the Sasanian past, from the Islamic caliphates, and from local Mesopotamian traditions. This is a distinctive archaeology that has to be understood in the wider context of the region, because doing so enriches our understanding of the complexity of the period.

One of the lasting legacies of the nineteenth century European approach to studying the past is a tendency to categorize communities. This is one of the reasons that the term "Byzantine" is so problematic; it automatically excludes those who do not fit our understanding of the dominant group. Many of these communities have been traditionally excluded from the narrative, but were connected by trade, faith, and/or imperial policies. Their exclusion sometimes lies in their geographical distance but it can also be due to the varying local languages (such as Syriac, Coptic, Armenian) and religious beliefs, which often separated them further from the Orthodox church (such as the Syriac churches in Mesopotamia). In other cases there were communities that technically fell under East Roman control (depending on the time frame), but which sat on the edge of the empire, including places like Sicily, Cyprus, and the Balkans. These were all regions deeply affected by both East Roman traditions as well as local ones. They also all had an important connection to trade routes. While all of these regions have traditionally been briefly alluded to in histories of the East Roman world, more recently excavation and survey is providing regional microhistories which enhance our understanding of the complexity of the wider medieval world. This becomes another place, then, where medieval becomes an appropriate and necessary term.

Communities on the Outside

When we consider communities "outside" the narrative of the East Roman Empire, we are largely dealing with those that are defined by three characteristics: language, faith, and liminality to Constantinople. While it is beyond the scope of this book to discuss all such communities in-depth, I will turn to three prominent ones here: the Syriac communities, the Armenians, and the Copts and offer three examples of places where archaeology can change the narrative of inclusion. All three communities were adjacent to the East Roman world (or within it, depending on the period), and held reciprocal relationships with it. It is difficult to argue that that they are entirely East Roman, but they were certainly affected by this heritage, and should be included in the wider medieval narrative. Unfortunately three barriers still restrict that inclusion in practice.

First, a linguistic barrier remains a huge deterrent in the scholarship, as all of these communities functioned within their own languages, all of which still tend to be the purview of small, specialized groups of scholars. This creates an invisible barrier that archaeology can transcend, although the material culture is often not considered. This problem is exacerbated by the fact that a large number of the original texts have never been translated into a modern language. Nevertheless, increasingly archaeologists are recognizing the importance of bringing these communities into the wider discussion of the East Roman world.

Second, the Christological controversies of the fifth and sixth centuries rendered these churches theologically different from the Byzantine Orthodox (and Catholic) worlds. The fifth century "Nestorian" controversy, although eventually dealt with in Byzantium, was to have far reaching consequences. First, there was the growth of the so-called Nestorian church in the Sasanian empire. Already an independent church before Nestorius's followers found refuge there, their belief in a Christ with two distinct natures (dyophysitism) further separated this church from the Orthodox Church and eventually lead to the creation of the East Syriac Church. This in turn was followed by the further solidification of Miaphysite beliefs (Christ having one indivisible nature) by the West Syriac, Armenian, and Coptic churches by the end of the fifth century, a decision that would have far reaching implications for these communities in dealing with Constantinople.[1] Even when these communities technically fell under the East Roman Empire as the Syriac Christians in Eastern Anatolia did, they remain separate entities in scholarship. In some ways this parallels the separation of Islamic and Christian archaeology in the Levant.

The third problem that separates these groups out from East Roman identity is their location under other empires, particularly in the later medieval period. By the start of the seventh century, Byzantium really refers, geographically, to Greece and Türkiye. Yet, many of these Christians continued

1 Dietmar W. Winkler, "The Syriac Church Denominations," in *The Syriac World*, ed. by Daniel King (Abingdon: Routledge, 2019), 119–33.

to either live just on the inside of the periphery of the East Roman world or to travel between and within it. However, the location of these communities under other empires also contributes to an artificial separation in scholarship. For the Syriac and Armenian Christians there was a long history of rule by first the Parthians, then the Sasanians, and finally the caliphate in Baghdad. The Copts fell under Muslim rule in the seventh century, yet remained one of the largest groups of Christians in the Near East throughout the Islamic period, and ones with strong connections to the West Syriac and Armenian communities. These were not isolated groups, and allowing for a wider understanding of multiple medieval archaeologies only underscores the complexity of the East Roman world in this period.

At the heart of the problem with all of this, of course, is that such separation and compartmentalization suggests that these groups did not speak to each other, and that there was no trade or interaction between them. But the reality of the period was quite different. Monks travelled between Egypt and northern Iraq, for example, and religious traditions and pilgrims moved along trade routes. Communities used local architectural traditions to express both their secular and religious activities, and these had far-reaching effects on the architecture of the East Roman world (such as the appearance of the dome). So, to leave them out creates a false narrative of religious and cultural uniformity in the East Roman world that needs to be challenged, which is precisely what archaeologists are able to do as we explore this material.

Of the archaeologies of the three communities presented here, Coptic archaeology is by far the most robust. The trajectory of Coptic archaeology is particularly fascinating, given that Egypt holds a place of privilege in the history of early Christianity as the birthplace of monasticism, and in archaeology generally as the home of the pharaohs. However, as Darlene Brooks Hedstrom has shown, the sense that was most prevalent among early Europeans who encountered Coptic material was disappointment, precisely because it did not fit into the same artistic narrative of the rest of the

East Roman world that could be seen in places like Constantinople and Ravenna. Yet, it had such a long history of being formative in the development of Christianity.[2] For Europeans, the pure Christian past was spoiled by a degraded, mud and stone version of monasticism that reflected, in European eyes, Eastern superstition and ignorance. Yet, until the coming of the Arabs, this material has still largely been seen as East Roman, albeit "more unusual than Late Antique contemporaries."[3]

In the last thirty years, the focus of medieval archaeology in Egypt has shifted in three ways which illustrate that it should be considered in comparison to more traditional East Roman sites. First, while work still continues primarily on religious structures, such as monasteries like the White Monastery, scholars are now thinking more about the social complexities of these communities. Thus, for example, scholars have begun to apply spatial analysis to the monastic landscape in Egypt, in order to consider how social communities were constructed within these monasteries. The work of Brooks Hedstrom, for example, particularly focuses on food and kitchens as part of the complex narrative of community. This is supported by a second shift which parallels movements in the Levant and other parts of the East Roman world to consider non-religious, non-elite communities. For example, there is increased study of how non-monastic communities functioned, such as the work at Trimithis in the Dakhla oasis.[4] This is a city which provides a microhistory of a site that incorporated both Roman and local elements, and thus

---

2 Brooks Hedstrom, *The Monastic Landscape of Late Antique Egypt* and Mary Horbury, "The British and the Copts," in *Views of Ancient Egypt Since Napoleon Bonaparte*, ed. David Jeffreys (London: University College of London Press, 2004), 153–70.

3 Brooks Hedstrom, *Monastic Landscape*, 53.

4 Paola Davoli, "Trimithis: A Case Study of Proto-Byzantine Urbanism" in *The Great Oasis of Egypt: The Kharga and Dakhla Oases in Antiquity*, ed. Roger S. Bagnall and Gaëlle Tallet (Cambridge: Cambridge University Press, 2019): 46–80.

provides a case study for understanding urban settlements in Egypt in comparison with other locations in the Late Roman period. Finally, scholars are focusing on connecting these communities, both monastic and secular, to communities outside of Egypt. For example, a project out of Leiden resulted in the understanding of the cultural interactions which occurred during the tenth and eleventh centuries, when there was intense contact between the West Syriac monks of northern Mesopotamia and the Coptic monks of Deir al-Surian.[5] For example, from the perspective of material culture Bas Snelders has shown that metalwork found in Egypt has distinct parallels with that manufactured around Mosul in northern Mesopotamia for both Christians and Muslims, indicating a transfer of goods as gifts during this period.

As Coptic archaeology mirrors the most important movements in East Roman archaeology, it should become a model for Syriac archaeology, a field which desperately needs more work. Archaeological exploration remains sparse outside of recording religious architecture; excavations are few and far between. For example, we still use the catalogue of extant churches in the Tur Abdin compiled by Gertrude Bell in the early twentieth century, and then updated by Marlia Mango. These primarily West Syriac churches are located in the eastern part of what is today modern Türkiye. Relatively limited archaeological work has been done on these structures since Bell, except for a multi-volume survey of the churches in the early 1980s and some articles on individual structures.[6] Yet, technically, the majority of these churches fell in the East Roman world. Similar problems exist for understanding the

---

5 See the collection of articles in Bas Ter Haar Romeny, *Religious Origins of Nations? The Christian Communities of the Middle East* (Leiden: Brill, 2010). For specific examples of interaction, see Snelders, *Identity and Christian-Muslim Interaction: Medieval Art of the Syrian Orthodox from the Mosul Area* (Leuven: Peeters, 2010).

6 Gernot Wiessner, *Christliche Kultbauten im Ṭūr ʿAbdīn* (Wiesebaden: Harrassowitz, 1982). While an important addition, Wiessner offered little in the way of dates of the structures he surveyed.

Church of the East. While outside of the East Roman world, there were connections between southern Mesopotamia and Eastern Anatolia, and these had lasting effects on theology and architecture. Yet, although there has been some excavation of a few churches, such as the 1920s discovery of the church at Ctesiphon, little has been done on the communities themselves. What remains shocking is the lack of archaeological work such as excavation or formal survey on the Syriac villages and monasteries in the region as a whole. The same has been true of the remains of the churches in northern Mesopotamia, which represent both East and West Syriac denominations.

Recent work while significant, is merely a drop in the bucket. The most recent scholarly work has still focused on architecture and epigraphy, with some singular excavation reports. For Mesopotamia, a new and much needed book by Elif Keser-Kayaalp looks at the architecture of northern Mesopotamia (including the excavations at Nisibis), while Amir Harrak has recorded the Syriac inscriptions in northern Iraq.[7] The publication from the work by *Kültürel Mirası Koruma Derneği* discussed at the start of this chapter is freely available, and provides some updated images of some of the churches in eastern Türkiye.[8] Beyond that, new work is being done by Iraqi archaeologists at al-Hira in southern Iraq, and increased work has been done on late medieval monastic sites stretching across the Silk Road into Western China.[9]

As Coptic archaeology is opening up new fields of research and connecting to the wider East Roman world, so we need to see the same in Syriac archaeologies. In order to illustrate this, I will turn to some examples from the West Syriac world

---

7 Elif Keser-Kayaalp, *Church Architecture of Late Antique Northern Mesopotamia* (Oxford: Oxford University Press, 2022), and Amir Harrak, *Syriac and Garshuni Inscriptions of Iraq*, Répertoire des inscriptions syriaques 2, 2 vols. (Paris: Académie des inscriptions et belles-lettres, 2010).

8 KMKD Syriac Project: https://intangiblesyriac.org/, July 10, 2024.

9 Martina Müller-Wiener et al., "Al-Hira Survey Project: Campaigns 2015–2018," *Sumer* 65 (2019): 87–110.

of where further questioning and archaeological exploration could substantially add to our understanding of the communities under the East Roman Empire. This is a community that had direct contact with the East Roman world to the west, the Armenians to the east, and the Sasanians and East Syriac Christians to the south. Theologically, it was connected to the Armenian and Coptic churches, and religious figures travelled between their respective monasteries.

While the ecclesiastical structures in the region are significant for understanding the role and form of religion, we have largely neglected the communal and domestic remains, which are extensive. This had long been a problem in East Roman archaeology until recently, but it is particularly acute in the Tur Abdin and northern Mesopotamia; it also means that we have traditionally classified an entire culture based on religious structures. The matter is becoming particularly urgent as many of these sites are disappearing. Here I draw your attention to the church of Yoldath Aloho in the Late Antique village of Serhavdana, which is known because of the remains of a Late Roman style carved arch.

What has remained outside the focus of earlier studies is that this church sits within the context of an entire enormous village which remains unsurveyed, unexcavated, and undated, but which stretches extensively over the hills surrounding the church. This village is just one of hundreds in the area that have never been fully documented, and are not being preserved or excavated.

A parallel situation can be seen in the site of Altintaş, which holds the remains of an important monastery, that of Mor Mushe, which was probably constructed between the ninth and eleventh centuries. Notable for its inscriptions and its complex architecture, what remains unremarked on is its proximity to a (probable) Islamic fortification or castle just to the northeast of the monastic complex, which probably dates to the eleventh or twelfth century.

Such a combination of structures suggests some cohabitation/interaction (whether friendly or otherwise) between communities, a fact which is generally noted in the Syriac

Figure 11. Church of Yoldath Aloho at Serhevdana. Photograph by author.

Figure 12. Village Remains at Serhevdana. Photograph by author.

Figure 13. Altintaş, with both monastery and castle. Photograph by author.

sources of the period such as the chronicle of Michael the Syrian. Understanding the Islamic structure is almost as difficult as understanding the Christian one, since, as noted earlier, little work has been done on these monuments either. Yet, here is a site that illustrates a place where we might be able to trace connections between the West Syriac community, the newly establish Turkic rulers, and the role of both on the border with the East Roman Empire.

The lack of conversation about these types of villages points to a wider issue in East Roman archaeology, one that has wide-ranging consequences. As one moves across Anatolia (and into Armenia), there are parallels that occur time and time again in the contexts of the small agricultural villages built throughout these regions. The ceramics are simple coarse wares, often decorated in similar ways with wavy line decoration; the wares are always local.

Domestic structures, while having different localized layouts, are made in similar ways of packed mud and stone. Material culture is represented by practical objects, like metal farm implements and cooking utensils. There are par-

Figure 14. Medieval ceramics, Altintaş. Photograph by author.

allels between them which suggest that we need to ask new questions about patterns of cooking and architecture that existed among rural communities in Anatolia and those further east. A number of small sites in eastern Türkiye that we would technically term East Roman, places like Gritille and Sos Höyük, present the same type of ceramics, for example, that are found at Çadır Höyük in central Anatolia or at sites in Armenia. A cursory glance at the ceramics at Altintaş shows the same sort of ceramics. This comparison is neither a claim that they are borrowing from one another, nor that the ceramics are representative of entire communities, but rather that there are new questions to be asked about foodways in the medieval period.[10] Indeed, a parallel argument for an Armenian village has also been made, since there is now

10 For new work on these kinds of questions, see Joanita Vroom, ed., *Feeding the Byzantine City: The Archaeology of Consumption in the Eastern Mediterranean* (Turnhout: Brepols, 2023).

increased excavation of small villages there.[11] While medieval ceramics are, as noted earlier, poorly understood, sites throughout Anatolia, including the Syriac east, provide an opportunity to consider how subsistence strategies changed in this period, and how this was reflected in ceramic production. A comparison of these ceramics would almost certainly allow us to consider food production and consumption in medieval rural contexts. These villages, whether Syriac, Armenian, or East Roman, have more in common with each other than they do with the cities of the period and are the key to understanding the lives of the rural population, something which we have seen has been extremely successful in medieval Greek archaeology.

The history of the study of medieval Armenia is characterized by some of the same trends as we have witnessed in relation to the Syriac communities. The earliest explorations of Armenia, however, came primarily from late nineteenth and early twentieth century French and Russian aristocratic interest in the major monuments like the church at Ani (now in Türkiye) and Zuart'noc'. While Armenia is opening up to further exploration, much of the literature outside of major works by figures like Charles Texier remains unknown to Western students because so much of the early archaeology is in Armenian and in Russian, due to its control of Armenia during the Soviet era.[12] What is clear is that the earliest work was really focused on the monumental architecture, again with little concern for surrounding villages or the continuity of the medieval period.

As with the Syriac material, Armenia is isolated from the East Roman world by its linguistic differences, its geographical distance, and by its theological stance. Yet, we know that

---

11 Kathryn Franklin, et al., "Examining the Late Medieval Village from the Case at Ambroyi, Armenia."

12 For an introduction, see Kleinbauer, *Early Christian and Byzantine Architecture*, xcix–cv and Ian Lindsay and Adam T. Smith, "A History of Archaeology in the Republic of Armenia," *Journal of Field Archaeology*, vol. 31 (2006):165–84.

Armenia was deeply connected to the political landscape of both the Late Roman and Sasanian empires. Further, the written sources tell us about Armenian saints and monks travelling through the countryside and interacting with East Roman religious figures in theological centres like Cappadocia. We know that there was interaction with the churches in the Tur Abdin as well. Between the ninth and eleventh centuries, Armenians played an important role in population and land exchanges in central Anatolia, and were pivotal to Crusader success in parts of Eastern Anatolia and Cilicia. This was not, then, a culture that was unconnected to the larger East Roman world, nor was it unimportant to the regional development of theological and liturgical differences in the medieval period. Yet, we keep this as a separate subfield, one that often is not connected to the larger medieval narrative.

The discussion of medieval Armenia has only recently begun to make its way into the archaeological discussion. While there has been archaeological investigation in Armenia, of course, the majority of it has focused on much earlier periods, as opposed to medieval sites. Most recently, Christina Maranci has begun to bring attention to this through the consideration of Armenian art and architecture, as for example in her study of Trdat, an architect who figures in the construction of churches in both Armenia and Byzantium.[13] Similarly, as noted above, Kathryn Franklin's archaeological work in Armenia has illustrated the same kinds of connections through comparisons with archaeological sites in eastern Türkiye. More recently, she has utilized the Silk Road to illustrate the connections between the East Roman empire and the Far East, via Armenia. Further it offers an important point of comparison with what we know about the Nestorians who travelled along the Silk Road during the late medieval period, thus opening up a wider concept of medieval archaeology.

13 Christina Maranci, "The Architect Trdat: Building Practices and Cross-Cultural Exchange in Byzantium and Armenia," *Journal of the Society of Architectural Historians*, vol. 62 (2003): 294–305.

One final point should be raised here. Both the Syriac and Armenian churches owe a substantial debt to the Sasanian world. This Persian Empire (226 CE–640 CE) is well known from the historical sources of the East Roman world, and much of these centre around the conflicts that the two empires were engaged in almost continuously. However, as with Seljuk archaeology, Sasanian archaeology is a cognate field that should be drawn into the discussion more carefully. While there is also need of more Sasanian archaeology, my point here is that what we do have is often not considered in relation to the development of communities in, particularly, northern Mesopotamia, Eastern Türkiye, or Armenia. Yet, the artistic and architectural traditions are present in these churches, and almost certainly had an effect on the material culture of all of these communities. Once again, a medieval archaeology would allow for more of this type of comparative work.

Communities on the Inside

While peripheral communities in the Near East have been traditionally excluded from the narrative for some of the reasons outlined above, European locations with strong East Roman connections have been underexplored as well. Contested island spaces like Cyprus and Sicily have been routinely oversimplified in analysis, or simply understudied in East Roman studies. Central Europe and the Balkans, which have a long and clear trajectory back to the Roman and Late Roman world, are also often sidelined, both because they are studied by a limited number of people (as in the case of the Syriac world) and, more problematically, because these histories have at times been misused in the name of nationalism. Yet, all of these spaces (and more that there is simply not room to discuss here, including North Africa, southern Russia, and coastal Italy) fell under the auspices of the East Roman Empire for portions of their histories and were all deeply influenced by the cultural traditions that evolved from the Roman world. They were also spaces of intense cultural interaction through trade and the arrival of new communities, something which reinforces their roles as independent microregions in the East Roman world.

Cyprus is perhaps the most central of all of these locations, and so serves as a good place to start the discussion. Luca Zavagno has written extensively about the archaeology of Cyprus in the medieval period, and he draws attention to the fact that scholars have oversimplified the history of the island as one of decline and ruralization, largely based on the primary sources which situated the arrival of the Arabs in the seventh century as a disaster for the island.[14] He stresses that earlier approaches to both the history and the archaeology were also influenced by contemporary events in Cyprus after the Turkish annexation of northern Cyprus which resulted in a lack of archaeology from that part of the island. Yet, as he says, seeing Cyprus in a negative light misses the point of the island, as it was vital to trade in the East Roman world, and was a place where ideas and goods passed through on a regular basis. It was, in short, an island of microregions:

> Indeed, we must consider that the fragmentation and localization of production and distribution provided Cyprus (as well as other islands, like Sicily, or coastal areas, like the southwest Anatolian coastline) with a unique chance to retain a far more complex economy as a middle ground between the economically coherent exchange circuits of Syria-Palestine and Egypt, the Byzantine capital, and the Aegean microregion.[15]

Each area of Cyprus responded differently to the events that unfolded throughout the early medieval period.

Recent archaeological exploration of various parts of Cyprus bears out Zavagno's observations that the earlier historiographical approach to Cyprus is perhaps too simplis-

---

14 Zavagno, *Cyprus between Late Antiquity and the Early Middle Ages*, 1–14.

15 Zavagno, *Cyprus between Late Antiquity and the Early Middle Ages*, 10.

tic. First, although the historical sources suggest a complete disaster for many communities in Cyprus after the relatively strong Late Roman period, the archaeological evidence does not entirely support this. Some sites on the coast were abandoned, and there was a decline in those populations. However, Marcus Rautman identifies new villages in the highlands being established, and that some of the cities continued to exist. Some of his argument hinges around the shift to locally made coarse wares, which can be identified for the seventh and eighth centuries, periods often seen as representing the abandonment of the island.[16] Nick Kardulis finds the same thing in his survey work in inland Cyprus. In short, as in most other areas of the East Roman world, the populations adjusted as changes affected the island, at times recreating villages in new locations, and at other points adapting. However, life continued on the island throughout the medieval period, including trade with the outside world.[17] During its regrowth after the ninth century, Cyprus was able to use its position in the centre of the Mediterranean to grow in importance once again. However, all of the excavators who have worked there in the last twenty years agree that it never really lost its prominence, regardless of the voices in the primary sources.

Sicily makes a good comparator to Cyprus, for many of the same reasons. Although less work has been done on Sicily than Cyprus, the key findings by primarily survey teams have come to largely the same types of conclusions as we see for Cyprus. That is, it is an island of microregions and microhistories, and must be approached on a case-by-case basis. Castrorao Barba, who has been working in other parts of medieval Italy, sees "Post-Roman Sicily...as a sort of case study for Mediterranean dynamics, connecting continuity, transformation, innovation and resilience to a wider frame of political change: the island's role in the Byzantine State,

---

16 Marcus Rautman, "The Villages of Byzantine Cyprus," in *Les villages dans l'empire byzantine*, ed. Lefort et al., 453–63.

17 Kardulias, "Adapting to the Cypriot Landscape," in *Spatialities of Byzantine Culture*, ed. Veikou and Nilsson, 262–87.

the Islamic conquest, the Norman domination, and the emergence of the Swabian empire."[18] As with Cyprus, the island shows continuity of trade networks and habitation throughout the medieval period, although often with adaptive changes to its role in the Mediterranean. Further, the arrival of Islamic communities did not seem to spell the end of the Christian ones, marking out a further form of adaptation.[19]

Finally, let us turn very briefly to the Balkans and Central Europe. This is a vast topic that cannot possibly be done justice here, but there are a couple of important observations to make about the region as an "inner" community that needs better inclusion. Christian Raffensperger has written extensively about the need for the inclusion of the Rus (and Eastern Europe) into the historical narrative of medieval Europe. Too often these groups sit on the outside of the definition of East Roman.[20] While there are misplaced nationalist trends that connect these regions to a glorified Byzantine Empire—ideas that have no basis in fact—the reality was that Central and Eastern Europe (including the Balkans generally) did serve as an important connector between Western Europe, Southern Europe, and the Near East. Moreover, it was a place through which ideas and trade travelled consistently throughout the medieval period.

As with Sicily, however, we are left with very limited archaeological evidence, which has led to overgeneralization about these regions. Terms like "barbarians" are often attached to the Balkans when we consider it in relation to the early East

---

18 Angelo Castrorao Barba and Giuseppe Mandalà, "Introduction," in *Suburbia and Rural Landscapes in Medieval Sicily*, ed. Castrorao Barba and Mandalà, vii.

19 See for example Alessandro Corretti and Claudio Filippo Mangiaracina, "Contessa Entellina: Rural vs. Urban Medieval Landscapes in Inner Western Sicily," in *Suburbia and Rural Landscapes in Medieval Sicily*, ed. Barba and Mandalà, 60–76.

20 Christian Raffensperger, "Reimagining Europe," in *The Medieval Networks of East Central Europe*, ed. Balasz Nagy, András Vadas, and Felicitas Schmeider (London: Routledge, 2018).

Roman world, and until the tenth and eleventh century, there were often images of violence associated with the communities in these regions. The primary sources are lacking, and the archaeology is again the purview of a very few scholars. That being said, however, there are some important trends that are beginning to come out of the survey and excavation that is being done. First, as with Cyprus and Sicily, archaeologists such as William Bowden and Florin Curta both argue for variation, both in terms of site use and development and in terms of populations. Secondly, the Balkans were not a monolithic entity, although this region too is often seen through the same lens of decline and abandonment as we have seen for other parts of the East Roman world, the reality is much more complex. For example, Curta has argued forcefully that the region needs to be understood as representing a number of different Slavic groups, and that better use needs to be made of the evidence that does exist. Thus, he argues that the presence of sixth century coin evidence for sites in the Balkans represents something quite different than it does in Anatolia. In Anatolia it speaks to an active trade economy and with its declining presence in the seventh century, a return to a more localized economy and the ruralization of the empire. In the Balkans, on the other hand, its continued presence speaks to the continuation of the Late Roman military in the region. He sees the small settlements as neither the hiding places of peasants, nor fortified settlements but rather as military controlled settlements that exemplify the complicated relationships the East Roman empire had with these communities.[21]

In short, all of these communities are characterized by their placement in the liminal space of the borders of the East Roman world. Yet, because they were in that space, the pop-

---

21 Curta, *The Making of the Slavs*; William Bowden, "A Window on an Uncertain World: Butrint and the Fortified Sites of Epirus in the 7th–9th Ceturies AD," in *Fortified Settlements in Early Medieval Europe: Defended Communities of the 8th–10th Centuries*, ed. N. Christie and H. Herold (Oxford: Oxbow, 2016), chap. 17.

ulations of all three had access to different influences than other parts of the East Roman world. For Sicily and Cyprus, much of this came through because of trade; for the Balkans, this was a world of everchanging populations. The excavations in all three regions show that there is no one size fits all approach to the East Roman world but that through careful analysis of microregions, we gain a sense of the complexity of social identity and site formation.

Conclusions

As I hope the material in this chapter illustrates, there is a real need to be more inclusive in terms of what we consider medieval East Roman archaeology. There are liminal communities which sit just inside, or indeed outside, the scope of what we would consider the East Roman world. The archaeology of these communities has in some ways been considered problematic, whether due to language or identity issues, or it has often been characterized with broad strokes as developing like other parts of the East Roman world. Important new research in most of these fields is showing that they must be approached as microregions, and in doing so we can better understand their relationships to Constantinople and to the other medieval communities they encountered. It widens the scope of the medieval lens, and helps to create a more inclusive view of the past. This matters because these people dealt with one another all the time in their own worlds and so we need to allow them the agency to do so in our interpretation of the past. While East Roman is perhaps an uncomfortable term for some of these regional archaeologies, the case can be made for understanding them in a wider medieval context.

Conclusions

In the end, why does any of what I have written above matter? As I write this book, I glance at the news. We are living in trying times. Increasingly we live in societies where people are not tolerant of difference, whether in our own countries or abroad, and people struggle to find common ground. Violence based in identity (religious and social) and dominance is, I think, depressing to any historian or archaeologist—we have seen it all before. Further, the medieval world has been used at times to justify violence and bigotry. Most notable, of course, is the lack of understanding of the crusades, which are generally presented as a Muslim versus Christian debacle. Little is understood about the contextual situation with al-Hakim in Egypt which led to the destruction of the Church of the Holy Sepulchre in Jerusalem; only that it was done. Little is understood about the social situation in Europe that allowed the pope to use what was, in essence, a political matter between Egypt and the Levant to send hordes of bored young men to the Middle East under the pretence of returning Jerusalem to the Christians. Rather, historical and modern conflicts are still understood in stark black and white terms in the modern world.

As historians, archaeologists, and students of the East Roman world, we understand that the history of the regions covered by the East Roman Empire was in fact never this simple, and that different religious, ethnic, and social populations existed alongside one another for centuries. They borrowed from one another, learned from one another, and, of course, they fought with one another. But their lived reality was a far cry from the stark historical divisions that we sometimes assume. We need to present this material in more nuanced ways, both to create more realistic narratives of the past and to do our part to combat modern perceptions of the past that are based on false narratives.

A description of modern pluralism from the Global Centre for Pluralism, funded in large part by the Aga Khan Foundation, provides, I think, a model of what our world should strive for:

> **Diversity in society is a universal fact**; how societies respond to diversity is a choice. Pluralism is a positive response to diversity. Pluralism involves taking decisions and actions, as individuals and societies, which are grounded in respect for diversity.
>
> We are living an historic moment of urgency for pluralism. Societies worldwide are being challenged to address issues of injustice, inequality and exclusion. When societies commit to becoming more just, peaceful and prosperous by respecting diversity and addressing systemic inequality, the impacts can be transformational. When the dignity of every individual is recognized, everyone feels they belong. We are all better off, for generations to come.[1]

While I am in no way saying that ancient or medieval societies fell under this modern description of pluralism, I *am* explicitly saying that we, as scholars of the Near East, have a role to play in ensuring that people understand that the stark divisions that societies lean on and often cite as having historical precedence never really existed. We have a role to play in creating true pluralism. The first line, though, has always been true.

By holding on to the old definitions of "Byzantine" archaeology, then, we contribute to an old narrative. This is a long-standing problem in the field, and has its origins in the start

---

1 Global Centre for Pluralism, "What is Pluralism?," https://www.pluralism.ca/who-we-are/, July 9, 2024.

of the discipline. It has created false divisions between religions, making it difficult to see the Christian communities that continued to exist in the Levant outside of churches and monasteries. And, finally, it has left whole populations out of the equation. To be fair, it has left the Muslims out of the context in these locations as well. At the root of all of this is a colonial belief that the history and archaeology of Christianity belongs to the West, and that we as scholars can pick and choose what we want to focus on to express that narrative.

Archaeology, however, cannot predict precisely what it will find. While it would be disingenuous to consider any archaeology to be completely objective, we do have a responsibility to understand that any material pulled out of the ground needs to be interpreted and published—and that we need to be more explicit about what this means about the way societies organized themselves. This means taking more theoretical stances, such as using life course theory or gender theory, to look at populations who have been underrepresented in the archaeological and historical narratives. It also means looking at the resilience of sites over the entire medieval period, regardless of who was in charge of the settlement officially. The shift from Christian to Muslim, or the inclusion of both, should be a more pertinent research question for all of us. It also means speaking out about the fact that there were multiple populations inhabiting the region throughout the medieval era; that is, we need to hear and present all the voices we come into contact with in this work. The medieval period in the East Roman world is uniquely situated for this because of the movement of populations due to environmental and social change.

It is impossible in a book of this length to talk about everything, but this should serve as a basis for further exploration of the field. East Roman archaeology has come a long way in the past thirty years, with the inclusion of more theoretical frameworks, with an understanding of the interplay of environmental and human factors, and with a move towards a microregional approach. In short, the field has moved away from the grand narratives of Empire but we still have a long way to go. On a practical level, we need to continue to work on the ceramics chronology for most regions, but especially for Anatolia. We need further comparative work in island archaeology, something I have barely touched here. We need to better understand the archaeology of cognate fields, such as Sasanian archaeology. We need more surveys in places like the Balkans and Anatolia. We need to compare evidence from the written sources with our archaeological material and we need to include the material from other languages and cultures (whether it be Arabic geographical texts or Syriac Chronicles). We need more scientific studies of bones and seeds and pollen. Essentially, we need more people to take up the field and to continue to push for its inclusion into the wider medieval narrative and into wider world history and archaeology.

This, then, is why the medieval archaeology of the East Roman world matters. As medieval archaeologists, we should shoulder the burden of a more equitable presentation of the past. In its own way, the medieval past was as interconnected as we are in the modern age and archaeology has the potential to illustrate that diversity.

Further Reading

In the following section, I have provided several key works per chapter that will provide good starting places for understanding the problems in medieval East Roman archaeology from Sicily to the borders of Iran. I have added comments where appropriate to explain the significance. I have avoided technical reports here, and instead have concentrated on texts that provide introductions to the problems and to several sites.

General

Byzas. Veröffentlichungen des Deutschen Archäologischen Instituts. Istanbul: Ege Yayınları, 2005.

*This series brings together different editors working on collections of articles around particular topics in material culture, such as pottery or tiles, and amasses important articles on understudied topics, often by active field archaeologists who are introducing new material. Although not specifically cited in this book, these volumes are invaluable to understand current trends in the field.

Crow, Jim. "Archaeology." In *The Oxford Handbook of Byzantine Studies*. Edited by Elizabeth Jeffreys, John Haldon, and Robin Cormack, 47–58. Oxford: Oxford University Press, 2008.

A brief introduction to East Roman/Byzantine archaeology in which Crow provides a succinct introduction to the field and its problems.

Kleinbauer, W. Eugene. *Early Christian and Byzantine Architecture: An Annotated Bibliography and Historiography*. Boston: Hall, 1992.

Although dated as a bibliography now, the historiographical elements of this make it an invaluable resource. The first part of the book, which provides a brief overview of the development of East Roman/Byzantine archaeology in each area is particularly important for understanding the development of the field.

Lefort, Jacques, Cécile Morrisson, and Jean-Perre Sodini, eds. *Les villages dans l'empire byzantine*. Paris: Lethielleux, 2005.

This is an outstanding collection of articles about rural villages throughout the East Roman world. Essential reading.

Ousterhout, Robert G. *Eastern Medieval Architecture: The Building Traditions of Byzantium and Neighboring Lands*. Onassis Series in Hellenic Culture. New York: Oxford University Press, 2019.

Ousterhout's recent introduction is a masterful survey of medieval architecture that takes into account some of the less understood areas, including Armenia, Egypt, and the Syriac East. It is a wonderful update to the older handbook by Richard Krautheimer. His use of the term medieval in the title is groundbreaking.

Said, Edward W. *Orientalism.* New York: Vintage, 1979.

This is a classic which has been both overused and vilified. Nevertheless, reading Said's ideas is imperative to understanding how the West has traditionally interacted with the Near East and its past.

Introduction

Anderson, William. "The Medieval Afterlife of Ancient Mounds." In *Context and Connection: Studies on the Archaeology of the Ancient Near East In Honour of Antonio Sagona*. Edited by A. G. Sagona et al., 359–79. Leuven: Peeters, 2018.

Because archaeological mounds are often associated with ancient cultures, the medieval material on the top has traditionally been ignored or oversimplified. Anderson introduces students of archaeology to the complexity of medieval usage of ancient sites. It is a useful article for understanding how Near Eastern sites work as well.

Decker, Michael J. "The Current State of Byzantine Archeology." *History Compass* 16, no. 9 (September 2018): e12459.

A brief introduction to the state of the field, with a call for more support for many of the reasons I have laid out in this book. Michael Decker was one of the first people to call for a reconsideration of Byzantine archaeology, and this article is essential.

Haldon, John, et al. "The Climate and Environment of Byzantine Anatolia: Integrating Science, History, and Archaeology." *The Journal of Interdisciplinary History* 45, no. 2 (2014): 113–61.

A key article on the importance of environmental science in East Roman archaeology.

Kaldellis, Anthony. *Romanland: Ethnicity and Empire in Byzantium*. Cambridge: Harvard University Press, 2019.

While not an archaeological text, this provides a superb introduction to the questions of identity in Byzantine studies. This has important ramifications for how we classify and consider medieval material. It is controversial in many ways, but Kaldellis's arguments have led to an important discussion in the field about how we define "Byzantine" generally.

Pettegrew, David K., William R. Caraher, and Thomas W. Davis, eds. *The Oxford Handbook of Early Christian Archaeology*. Oxford: Oxford University Press, 2019.

Introduction to Early Christian archaeology, with excellent chapters on regional archaeologies.

Stewart, Michael Edward, David Alan Parnell, and Conor Whately, eds. *The Routledge Handbook on Identity in Byzantium*. Abingdon: Routledge, 2022.

A recent set of articles on rethinking identity in Byzantine/East Roman studies.

Stouraitis, Yannis. *Identities and Ideologies in the Medieval East Roman World*. Edinburgh: Edinburgh University Press, 2022.

Another important collection of essays which raise new questions about the identities we have assigned to the East Roman past.

Veikou, Myrto, and Ingela Nilsson, eds. *Spatialities of Byzantine Culture from the Human Body to the Universe*. Leiden: Brill, 2022.

A key collection of essays on the spatial turn in East Roman archaeology. One of very few theoretically based volumes, and many of the articles represent cutting-edge research in the field.

Chapter 1

Decker, Michael J. *The Byzantine Dark Ages*. Debates in Archaeology. London: Bloomsbury Academic, 2016.

A good introduction by an archaeologist to the problems of how we define the period between the seventh and ninth centuries.

Foss, Clive. *History and Archaeology of Byzantine Asia Minor*. Aldershot: Variorum, 1990.

The collected essays of one of the formative archaeologists in the field. Essential reading to understand how the field developed.

Roberts, Neil et al., "Not the End of the World? Post-Classical Decline and Recovery in Rural Anatolia." *Human Ecology* 46, no. 3 (June 2018): 305–22.

An important introduction to the topic of oversimplifying decline and recovery in Byzantine archaeology, and the importance of interdisciplinary research in creating a complete picture of the period.

Whittow, Mark. "Early Medieval Byzantium and the End of the Ancient World." *Journal of Agrarian Change* 9, no. 1 (2009): 134–53.

This was one of the most formative articles for my own research. Whittow argues for this period as one of change, and claims that we are doing a disservice by not paying enough attention to it, particularly in Anatolia.

Chapter 2

Haldon, John, Hugh Elton, and Jim Newhard. *Archaeology and Urban Settlement in Late Roman and Byzantine Anatolia: Euchaïta-Avkat-Beyözü and Its Environment*. Cambridge: Cambridge University Press, 2018.

This is a model publication for understanding how both urban and rural societies changed between the Roman, Late Roman and early medieval period. As well, it provides a good example of how much information can be gained from survey.

McCormick, Michael, et al., "Climate Change during and after the Roman Empire: Reconstructing the Past from Scientific and Historical Evidence." *Journal of Interdisciplinary History* 43, no. 2 (2012): 169–220.

An introduction to the role of interdisciplinary research around climate in relation to the Late Roman world in Europe.

Magnússon, Sigurður Gylfi. "Views into the Fragments: An Approach from a Microhistorical Perspective." *International Journal of Historical Archaeology* 20, no. 1 (March 2016): 182–206.

An important introduction to the concept of microhistory and its role in understanding medieval societies.

Mímisson, Kristján, and Sigurður Gylfi Magnússon. "Singularizing the Past: The History and Archaeology of the Small and Ordinary." *Journal of Social Archaeology* 14, no. 2 (June 2014): 131–56.

This is an extension of the article above in that it extends the concept of microhistory to archaeology through a process called singularization.

Niewöhner, Philipp, ed. *The Archaeology of Byzantine Anatolia: From the End of Late Antiquity until the Coming of the Turks*. New York: Oxford University Press, 2017.

A recent introduction to the major excavations and survey projects in Türkiye in the past twenty years. This also provides an important overview of topics such as coins, ceramics and fortifications. It is an invaluable source for wider bibliography in the field. This volume provides introductions to sites that have few technical publications in English as well.

Redman, Charles L., and Ann P. Kinzig, "Resilience of Past Landscapes: Resilience Theory, Society, and the *Longue durée*." *Conservation Ecology* 7, no. 1 (2003): 14 [online].

This is essential reading to understanding the use of resilience theory in archaeology.

Vionis, Athanasios K, Jeroen Poblome, and Marc Waelkens. "The Hidden Material Culture of the Dark Ages: Early Medieval Ceramics at Sagalassos (Turkey): New Evidence (ca. AD 650–800)." *Anatolian Studies* 59 (2009): 147–65.

This is a paper that stresses the importance of the chronology of the coarse wares in the post-Roman period.

Vroom, Joanita. *Byzantine to Modern Pottery in the Aegean: 7th to 20th Century: An Introduction and Field Guide*. 2nd rev ed. Turnhout: Brepols, 2014.

This is the best handbook for understanding and dating East Roman fine wares in the Aegean.

Chapter 3

Bintliff, J. L. *The Complete Archaeology of Greece from Hunter-Gatherers to the 20th Century AD*. Chichester: Wiley-Blackwell, 2012.

Although a textbook, the chapters on Greek medieval archaeology provide an excellent introduction to the field.

Gerstel, Sharon E. J. *Rural Lives and Landscapes in Late Byzantium: Art, Archaeology, and Ethnography*. Cambridge: Cambridge University Press, 2015.

Gerstel uses a wide range of evidence to illustrate how we can trace the continuous use of Greek villages in the Late Medieval period, and what this can tell us about the people and societies that lived in them.

Izdebski, Adam, and Michael Mulryan, eds. *Environment and Society in the Long Late Antiquity.* Leiden: Brill, 2019.

An important collection of papers on new movements in environmental archaeology in the Late Antique period.

Kondyli, Fotini. *Rural Communities in Late Byzantium: Resilience and Vulnerability in the Northern Aegean.* Cambridge: Cambridge University Press, 2022.

Provides an account of the survey of two Greek islands and the evidence for how villages sustained themselves throughout this period.

Kondyli, Fotini, and Benjamin Anderson, eds. *The Byzantine Neighbourhood: Urban Space and Political Action.* London: Routledge, 2021.

An important collection of papers that offers new consideration of how we look at Byzantine space and neighbourhoods. Extremely important for developing social theory.

Sanders, Guy. "Problems in Interpreting Rural and Urban Settlement in Southern Greece, AD 365–700." In *Landscapes of Change: Rural Evolutions in Late Antiquity and the Early Middle Ages.* Edited by Neil Christie. 163–93. Abingdon: Routledge, 2016.

An important theoretical article on the variations between site types in southern Greece by the former director of the Corinth excavations.

Chapter 4

Avni, Gideon. *The Byzantine-Islamic Transition in Palestine: An Archaeological Approach.* Oxford: Oxford University Press, 2014.

Avni introduces the transition period in Palestine and draws attention to both the differences visible between villages, and the places where communities interacted with one another.

Eger, A. Asa, ed. *The Archaeology of Medieval Islamic Frontiers: From the Mediterranean to the Caspian Sea*. Denver: University Press of Colorado, 2019.

A recent collection of articles detailing precisely the connections happening on the frontiers of the Islamic world. Essential reading.

Eger, A. Asa. *The Islamic-Byzantine Frontier: Interaction and Exchange Among Muslim and Christian Communities*. London: Tauris, 2015.

Eger is one of the first scholars to draw attention to the interaction occurring between the empires, arguing for a more complex set of negotiations and living arrangements than we have previously believed.

Magness, Jodi. *The Archaeology of the Early Islamic Settlement in Palestine*. Winona Lake: Eisenbrauns, 2003.

Essential reading on early Islamic Palestine.

Walmsley, Alan. *Early Islamic Syria*. London: Bloomsbury, 2013.

This offers some interesting reconsiderations of the way we have looked at the transition period and early Islamic material in Syria, including in relation to the Dead Cities.

Chapter 5

Armenia

Franklin, Kathryn J., et al. "Examining the Late Medieval Village from the Case at Ambroyi, Armenia." *Journal of Near Eastern Studies* 76, no. 1 (2017): 113–38.

This is an important article that illustrates how much these Armenian villages had in common with other villages in eastern Türkiye.

Maranci, Christina. "The Architect Trdat: Building Practices and Cross-Cultural Exchange in Byzantium and Armenia." *Journal of the Society of Architectural Historians* 62, no. 3 (2003): 294–305.

Maranci is one of the foremost scholars of Armenia, and this is an introduction to her work which illustrates exactly how much interaction there was between Byzantium and Armenia.

Balkans

Christie, Neil, and Hajnalka Herold, eds. *Fortified Settlements in Early Medieval Europe: Defended Communities of the 8th–10th Centuries*. Oxford: Oxbow, 2016.

An important collection of articles that includes several on central Europe.

Curta, Florin. *The Making of the Slavs: History and Archaeology of the Lower Danube Region, c. 500–700*. Cambridge: Cambridge University Press, 2001.

An important introduction to the early archaeology of the Slavs.

Coptic

Badawy, Alexander. *Coptic Art and Archaeology: The Art of the Christian Egyptians from the Late Antique to the Middle Ages*. Cambridge, MA: MIT, 1978.

A dated work, but still useful as a general survey.

Brooks Hedstrom, Darlene L. *The Monastic Landscape of Late Antique Egypt: An Archaeological Reconstruction*. Cambridge: Cambridge University Press, 2017.

The most significant new addition to the archaeology of the Coptic world. The first two chapters offer important insight into the historiographical problems of Egypt.

Cyprus

Zavagno, Luca. *Cyprus between Late Antiquity and the Early Middle Ages (ca. 600–800): An Island in Transition*. London: Routledge, 2017.

*An excellent summary and analysis of the work done in Cyprus, with an important new set of conclusions and approaches.

Sicily

Barba, Angelo Castrorao, and Gabriele Castiglia. *Perspectives on Byzantine Archaeology: From Justinian to the Abbasid Age (6th–9th centuries AD)*. Turnhout: Brepols, 2022.

An excellent collection of essays that is wide-ranging in its geographical focus.

Barba, Angelo Castrorao, and Giuseppe Mandalà, eds. *Suburbia and Rural Landscapes in Medieval Sicily*. Oxford: Archeopress, 2023.

An excellent collection of articles, many of which touch on locations that are generally lacking in the historical narratives.

Syriac Communities

Bell, Gertrude Lowthian, and Marlia Mundell Mango. *The Churches and Monasteries of the Ṭur'Abdin*. London: Pindar, 1982.

*Although dated, this is the earliest source for the churches of this region. Some of the plans are still in use, and for some structures, these are the only extant descriptions still available. Mundell Mango's update is essential.

Keser Kayaalp, Elif. *Church Architecture of Late Antique Northern Mesopotamia*. Oxford: Oxford University Press, 2021.

*The most recent work on the Syriac churches in northern Mesopotamia, Keser Kayaalp draws on recent excavations and surveys, and it is an important update to Bell's work.

Printed in the United States
by Baker & Taylor Publisher Services